CAPTURING SOLUTIONS FOR LEARNING AND SCALING UP

Documenting Operational Experiences for Organizational Learning and Knowledge Sharing

Steffen Soulejman Janus

© 2017 International Bank for Reconstruction and Development / The World Bank
1818 H Street NW, Washington, DC 20433
Telephone: 202-473-1000; Internet: www.worldbank.org

Some rights reserved

1 2 3 4 20 19 18 17

This work is a product of the staff of The World Bank with external contributions. The findings, interpretations, and conclusions expressed in this work do not necessarily reflect the views of The World Bank, its Board of Executive Directors, or the governments they represent. The World Bank does not guarantee the accuracy of the data included in this work. The boundaries, colors, denominations, and other information shown on any map in this work do not imply any judgment on the part of The World Bank concerning the legal status of any territory or the endorsement or acceptance of such boundaries.

Nothing herein shall constitute or be considered to be a limitation upon or waiver of the privileges and immunities of The World Bank, all of which are specifically reserved.

Rights and Permissions

This work is available under the Creative Commons Attribution 3.0 IGO license (CC BY 3.0 IGO) http://creativecommons.org/licenses/by/3.0/igo. Under the Creative Commons Attribution license, you are free to copy, distribute, transmit, and adapt this work, including for commercial purposes, under the following conditions:

Attribution—Please cite the work as follows Janus, Steffen Soulejman. 2017. *Capturing Solutions for Learning and Scaling Up: Documenting Operational Experiences for Organizational Learning and Knowledge Sharing.* Washington, DC: World Bank. doi: 10.1596/978-1-4648-1114-2. License: Creative Commons Attribution CC BY 3.0 IGO

Translations—If you create a translation of this work, please add the following disclaimer along with the attribution: *This translation was not created by The World Bank and should not be considered an official World Bank translation. The World Bank shall not be liable for any content or error in this translation.*

Adaptations—If you create an adaptation of this work, please add the following disclaimer along with the attribution: *This is an adaptation of an original work by The World Bank. Views and opinions expressed in the adaptation are the sole responsibility of the author or authors of the adaptation and are not endorsed by The World Bank.*

Third-party content—The World Bank does not necessarily own each component of the content contained within the work. The World Bank therefore does not warrant that the use of any third-party-owned individual component or part contained in the work will not infringe on the rights of those third parties. The risk of claims resulting from such infringement rests solely with you. If you wish to re-use a component of the work, it is your responsibility to determine whether permission is needed for that re-use and to obtain permission from the copyright owner. Examples of components can include, but are not limited to, tables, figures, or images.

All queries on rights and licenses should be addressed to World Bank Publications, The World Bank Group, 1818 H Street NW, Washington, DC 20433, USA; e-mail: pubrights@worldbank.org.

ISBN (paper): 978-1-4648-1114-2
ISBN (electronic): 978-1-4648-1115-9
DOI: 10.1596/978-1-4648-1114-2

Branding: Vladimir Herrera
Graphic design: Greg Wlosinski, World Bank Group General Services Department, Printing & Multimedia

Library of Congress Cataloging-in-Publication Data has been requested

CONTENTS

About This Guide	v
Acknowledgments	vii
About the Author	viii
Introduction	1
Step 1. Identification	9
Step 2. Capturing	19
Step 3. Validation	37
Step 4. Formatting	45
Step 5. Packaging for Learning and Scaling Up	51
Appendixes	63
Glossary	112
References	116

ABOUT THIS GUIDE

A volcano on the Indonesian island of Java has erupted. Suddenly, local and federal officials must make life-and-death decisions in rapid succession about this disaster in this time and place: How to organize emergency communications, and through which channels? How to evacuate people, and into which shelters? How to manage emergency health care? How to coordinate volunteers and provide emergency food, water, and other essentials?

These must be informed decisions, based on the latest knowledge of what works, why, and in what circumstances. Successful organizations equip their staff with the right knowledge at the right time for best results. But if it is to be shared at the right moment with the right person, knowledge must first be identified. And then it must be put down on paper or otherwise recorded so it will be accessible beyond a limited group.

Not all organizational challenges are matters of life or death, but staff members around the world are making critical decisions every day. Access to peer knowledge gained from previous experiences can lead to better decisions.

This step-by-step guide describes how to systematically capture knowledge from such operational experiences and use it to inform decision making and support professional learning. The captured lessons and takeaways are documented as knowledge assets, discrete and consistently formatted documents that present answers to one specific question or challenge.

But what sounds like a simple idea is not always easy to achieve. It requires leaders who want to orient the entire organization and all of its operational activities to the goal of learning from experience and replicating successes. Creating such an organization—creating the policies and governance structures related to knowledge sharing and learning, developing the skills required to carry out knowledge sharing, and monitoring and evaluating the performance of the knowledge-sharing endeavor—is the subject of the World Bank's comprehensive handbook Becoming a Knowledge-Sharing Organization.[1]

In the present guide, we assume that the bulk of the work discussed in the handbook has already taken place. Here instead we cover in more detail the process of creating the knowledge asset, the central element needed for learning. As summarized in chapters 5 and 6 of Becoming a Knowledge-Sharing Organization, creating

---

[1] Steffen Soulejman Janus, *Becoming a Knowledge-Sharing Organization: A Handbook for Scaling Up Solutions through Knowledge Capturing and Sharing* (Washington, DC: World Bank, 2016).

a knowledge asset consists five specific, largely technical steps in which your organization (1) identifies, (2) captures, (3) validates, (4) prepares for dissemination, and finally (5) uses operational lessons learned for sharing and replication. The chapters and appendixes of this guide are devoted to the details of these five steps and provide practical tools, templates, and checklists to help you accomplish each one.

The intended audience for this guide includes professionals, midlevel managers, knowledge and learning experts, and IT specialists, particularly those in the public sector of developing countries. It also includes consultants who may be hired by an organization to perform some of these functions.

The information in this guide is based on years of work—by the Organizational Knowledge Sharing program in the World Bank Institute and the World Bank's Leadership, Learning, and Innovation Vice Presidency—in collaboration with public sector agencies in numerous developing countries around the world. It distills our learning and theirs in the hopes that your organization can likewise see its public service become increasingly effective.

ACKNOWLEDGMENTS

I thank my colleagues in the Knowledge Sharing program at the World Bank, whose extensive and productive work with country institutions helped fine-tune the strategies presented here. Special thanks go to Mathy Vanbuel and Nicolas Meyer for their aid in shaping some of the important early ideas for this book; and to Robin v. Kippersluis and Divya Gupta, who contributed examples of their work on sanitation in India.

I am grateful to Laurent Besançon, Oscar de Bruyn Kops, and Roby Senderowitsch for their invaluable support and encouragement.

I am also grateful to the experts who graciously agreed to review the manuscript: Oscar de Bruyn Kops, Han Fraeters, Sahr Kpundeh, Silvia Malgioglio, Anand Rajaram, Vincent Ribiere, and Monika Weber-Fahr. This handbook is the richer for their valuable insights and thoughtful comments.

My own work on this book would not have been possible without the support my loving family has so generously given to me. They have my deepest gratitude.

Steffen Soulejman Janus
Spring 2017

ABOUT THE AUTHOR

Steffen Soulejman Janus manages the Knowledge Sharing program in the World Bank's vice presidency for Equitable Growth, Finance, and Institutions. There, he conceived and developed the World Bank's offerings of organizational knowledge-sharing methods to public sector institutions and senior management teams across the world. In parallel, he manages innovative social development projects focused on improving the livelihoods of the poor and disadvantaged. Steffen, who received a master's degree in business administration from Columbia University, was an initiator of the African Platform for Development Effectiveness and is a board member of the Global Development Learning Network. He is the author of the World Bank handbook, *Becoming a Knowledge-Sharing Organization*.

INTRODUCTION

Why Is Knowledge Retention and Sharing Important?

From the earliest moments in our childhood, we learned through experience. When we learned how to walk, it was through a process of falling and getting up again and again. Our professional lives are also mostly built on learning from experience. Our daily work consists of performing tasks intended to yield some output—with results that are sometimes successful, sometimes not. We remember such experiences, especially when things went wrong.

Organizations learn, too, but some do a better job of it than others. Those that are the most successful at it are referred to as learning organizations or knowledge-sharing organizations. They establish systems and processes to ensure that they preserve experiences that led to negative outcomes and build on those that led to success.

> Strengthening institutions' knowledge-sharing capabilities can profoundly affect the speed and efficiency with which progress is consolidated, scaled up, and replicated.

After all, there are only two ways to learn about solutions to a particular problem or challenge: directly turning to experts and stakeholders or going through materials that have documented the particular experience and solution path. Because experts on the problem you are facing right now are not likely to be available, access to documented solutions is critical.

The organizational capacity to learn is enormously important for public institutions in developing countries. Over the past decades, they have accumulated a wealth of positive and negative experience in boosting growth and prosperity. Unfortunately, institutions usually did not have the intention or ability to retain and share their experiences, and many important lessons were lost along the way. Strengthening institutions' knowledge-sharing capabilities can profoundly affect the speed and efficiency with which progress is consolidated, scaled up, and replicated.

The Place of Knowledge Capturing in a Learning Organization

Before we turn to the subject of knowledge capturing and learning from experience, let's place it within the broader context of the knowledge-sharing organization (as presented in more detail in the World Bank handbook Becoming a Knowledge-Sharing Organization).

For knowledge sharing to thrive, organizations need to develop capabilities at two levels: (1) the enabling environment for knowledge sharing and (2) technical skills. Hence, becoming a knowledge-sharing organization involves a complex change management process. A complete organizational transformation involves initiatives in eight areas, or pillars (figure I.1).

The left side of figure I.1—the "enabling environment"—concerns the management strategy and policies; the right side—"technical skills"—deals with the technical capacity to implement effective knowledge capturing and sharing.

This guide addresses the first two of the technical skill areas shown in figure I.1. It provides tools and guidance to systematically (1) identify and capture operational experiences and lessons learned and (2) turn these experiences into knowledge and learning offerings.[2]

The knowledge being captured, turned into shareable assets, and used for learning is knowledge that initially resides only in people's heads—that is, knowledge based on personal experience that has not previously been documented in a shareable format. We do not address existing documents and publications, which are considered explicit knowledge.

Capturing knowledge provides the content for two resources that are essential to a learning and knowledge-sharing organization:

» A comprehensive knowledge library that works as a question and answer (Q&A) system to inform just-in-time learning and rapid decision making
» A set of learning tools, such as workshops, presentations or trainings that equip an organization's staff (and other stakeholders) to perform operational tasks informed by previous experiences

A Five-Step Process

Our experience and that of our clients has shown that capturing and preparing knowledge assets can best be seen as five distinct yet closely interrelated steps: (1) knowledge identification, (2) capturing, (3) validation, (4) preparation for dissemination (also referred to as "formatting"), and (5) use in learning. The suggested sequence will not always match the needs of every organization or the content of every potential knowledge asset. Nor are the steps completely distinct; for example, validation should happen throughout the process, and preparation for dissemination can occur during the capturing step. We do, however, suggest explicitly building all five steps into your organization's knowledge management system.

---

[2] Just as the present guide treats the first two skill areas in figure I.1 in greater detail than does the handbook, the World Bank's 2015 guide *The Art of Knowledge Exchange* addresses the third skill area—knowledge sharing.

Figure I.1 Eight Pillars Supporting a Knowledge-Sharing Organization

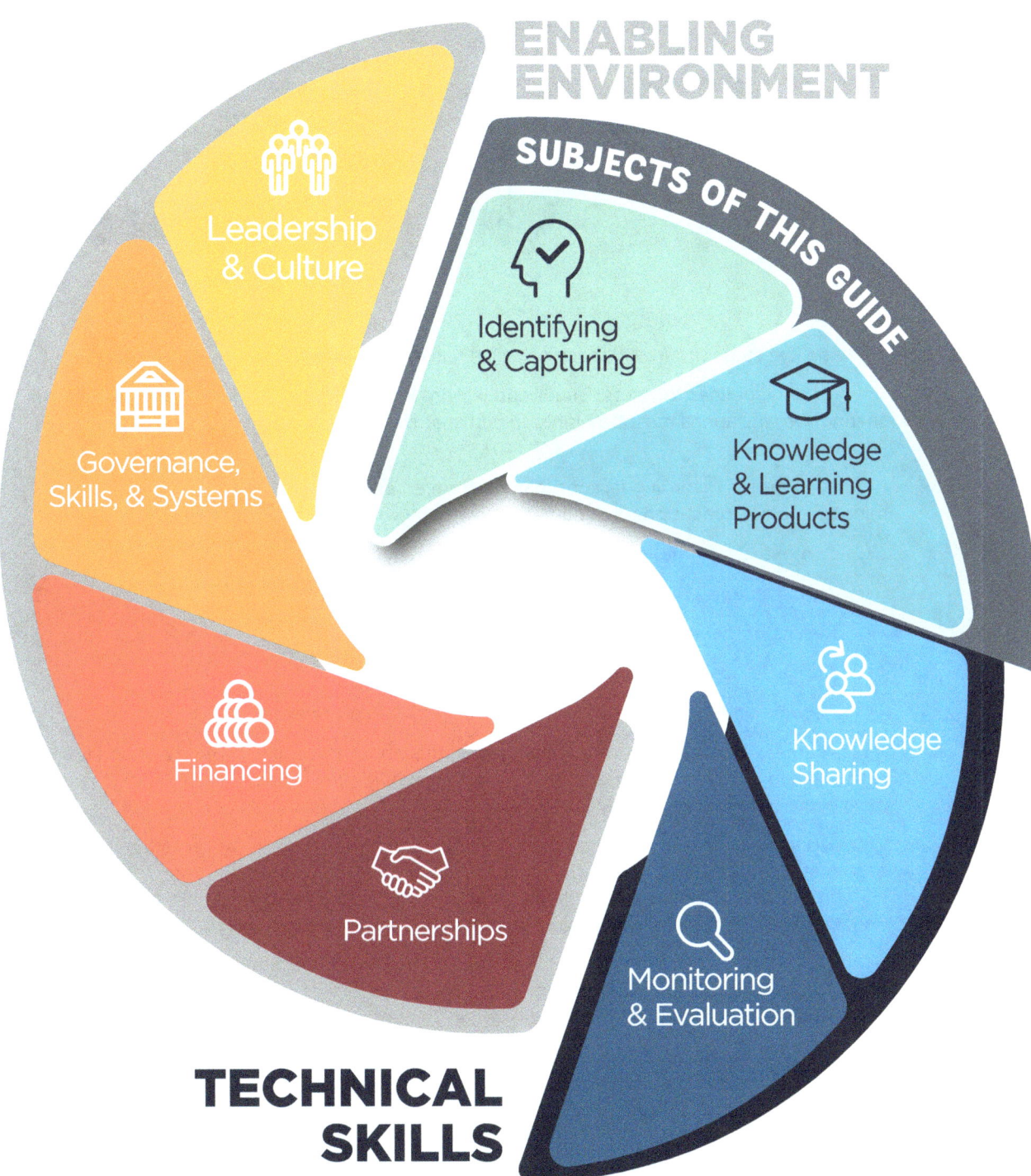

Figure I.2 The Five Steps for Learning from Solutions

Let's preview the five steps (figure I.2), each of which has its own chapter.

1. **Identification** defines the experiences and lessons learned that should be captured for later sharing. Organizations must be highly selective at this stage to avoid wasting valuable time and resources.

2. **Capturing** means recording lessons learned from an experience or event. Using a predetermined template, practitioners document knowledge with a standardized story line:

    - Contextual information
    - Actual actions undertaken to overcome the challenge
    - Results of the actions
    - Critical lessons learned from the experience
    - Recommendations for those interested in replicating the experience elsewhere

3. **Validation** ensures that captured knowledge is presented truthfully, correctly, and in a professional and accessible manner. While validation should ideally happen during all stages, it must occur before using a knowledge asset.

4. **Formatting** involves applying a common, consistent, and user-friendly presentation standard, or format, to all assets so that users can quickly and efficiently browse through them—especially important for assets containing a variety of media; and labeling assets with information, keywords, and other metadata to increase their searchability.

5. **Use in learning** refers to (1) transforming a discrete knowledge asset into a knowledge or learning product, such as a publication, presentation, or case study and (2) designing learning activities around that product to engage an audience.

Capturing Experiences and Lessons Learned for Scaling Up in Indonesia, India, and Nigeria: How Three Developing-Country Institutions Became Learning Organizations

A number of organizations and development programs have made big strides in using knowledge sharing to improve their effectiveness. In the following boxes, we introduce three examples of institutions using systematic documentation to inspire others—both inside and outside their organizations—to replicate or adapt their problem-solving approaches: Indonesia's National Disaster Management Authority (BNPB), India's Swachh Bharat Mission (SBM), and Nigeria's Lagos Metropolitan Area Transport Authority (LAMATA). You will encounter one or more of these institutions again in subsequent chapters, where their experiences in dealing with each of the five steps provide real-life context.

Indonesia's National Disaster Management Authority (BNPB)

Every year, more than 600,000 people in Indonesia suffer from earthquakes, flooding, landslides, and tsunamis. Between 2000 and 2010, these natural disasters cost the country an estimated 0.3 percent of GDP per year.

Managing and building resilience to these threats are top agenda items for the government of Indonesia, which has had a disaster management office in one form or another since 1966. The current agency, BNPB, was launched in 2008 and reports directly to the president of Indonesia, who appoints its chairman. As befits the far-flung nature of the threats, BNBP operates through a network of 500 provincial and municipal disaster management agencies (BPBDs) and NGOs.

BNPB quickly realized that dealing effectively with its enormous task would a disaster preparedness program based on know-how and lessons learned from past experience.

First, BNPB leadership **agreed on a vision** of the agency as an efficient knowledge-sharing institution for disaster management, providing innovative and effective disaster management solutions not only for Indonesia but regionally and globally. To implement this vision, the leadership **developed a knowledge-management policy,** instituted a task force with members from all operational departments to oversee the execution of the policy, and **budgeted for support** of a knowledge program. It also developed a strong set of **incentives** for employees and organizational partners to capture mission-critical experiences and contribute to a national knowledge pool on disaster management.

> continued

> continued from the previous page

Second, BNPB has **issued a national regulation** (Perka) mandating systematic knowledge capturing and sharing in the field of disaster management—a global first. Perka sets out principles, knowledge-sharing activities, and guidelines for implementation. Knowledge-capturing teams are learning common standards for the five steps of capturing and preparing knowledge assets.

Third, BNPB's senior management **recognized the need for strategic partnerships** with think tanks, universities, and other domestic and international partners to support systematic knowledge capture and sharing.

Fourth, BNPB **established a central knowledge library** of Indonesia's disaster management experiences to guide responses to future events and provide training material. It is web accessible from smartphones and computers via the "Disaster Management Solutions Finder," an application that permits searches of the library's contents, includes GPS location data and mapping, and allows users to contact the experts who contributed to any particular knowledge asset.

Fifth, it **expanded the capacity of its training center** in Jakarta through distance-learning formats such as videoconferencing and web-based e-learning. The training center has also started to localize its offerings by adopting Indonesian experiences as case studies for learners.

Systematically capturing and sharing operational lessons learned has been yielding important outcomes, including improved flood preparedness in remote areas and successful practices for creating livelihoods after volcano eruptions.

These new capabilities are enabling BNPB to retain important operational knowledge and develop critical institutional memory, scale up lessons learned through national knowledge-sharing mechanisms, and conduct strategic South-South knowledge exchanges with peer disaster management agencies in other countries. BNPB's knowledge-sharing capacity is thus working internally, domestically, and internationally.

India's Swachh Bharat Mission (SBM)

Every day, 500 children die in India from diarrheal diseases; 22 million girls do not have access to toilets at school; and more than 6% of the country's GDP is lost due to poor sanitation. Hygiene is one of India's most urgent development challenges. The government of India has launched the Swachh Bharat Mission (Clean India Mission) to stop open defecation and achieve universal sanitation by 2019. This ambitious goal assumes **a massive change in sanitation behavior** for the 600 million Indians—more than half the population—who currently defecate in the open.

To help tackle this challenge, the SBM, together with the World Bank, embarked on a journey to use **systematic knowledge capturing and sharing to change behavior.** The components of the project included identification, capturing, validation, and packaging of local sanitation solutions (institutional, behavioral, and technical). It required **better collaboration and adaptive learning** among project implementers, government agencies, and partners. And the goal was effective sharing and replication of good practices and solutions at scale within and between states and at the national level.

Using the World Bank's methods of organizational knowledge sharing, the SBM team developed a comprehensive approach to **build local capacities** for continuous identification, capture, validation, and packaging of local sanitation solutions. To ensure that the solutions were not one-off or project-limited, they had to be institutionalized at all levels, including the national Ministry of Drinking Water and Sanitation, state government departments, and local communities.

Given the limited literacy of many rural community members, facilitators and sanitation officials were trained in documenting sanitation solutions with video so that knowledge could be communicated through story telling.

Through a participatory process the team designed and developed a platform, the SBM Solutions Finder, to **host the captured lessons and make them accessible online and with an app.** The platform is anchored in the Ministry of Drinking Water and Sanitation to make sure local sanitation solutions are leveraged nationally.

As a result, the ministry and three states (Haryana, Rajasthan, and Uttar Pradesh) have **initiated systematic processes of knowledge capturing and sharing.** More than 50 local sanitation solutions have been documented in the first half-year of the engagement, and the number of communities following the approach is quickly rising. Intrastate knowledge exchanges in two states (Haryana and Uttar Pradesh) have inspired officials and allowed them to learn from good practices and successful local solutions to scale up SBM implementation. Other states have expressed interest in joining the capturing and sharing process.

Nigeria's Lagos Metropolitan Area Transport Authority (LAMATA)

LAMATA is a semiautonomous agency established in 2002 to deliver public transportation in the Lagos metropolitan area, by far the largest metro area in Africa. It is part of the Lagos Urban Transport Project (LUTP), which was funded by the World Bank to bring to the state of Lagos efficient public transportation that is accessible to all, helps reduce poverty, provides economic opportunities, and promotes viable communities. LAMATA opened Nigeria's first bus rapid transit (BRT) line in 2008 and is working on the initial segment of its first modern light rail transit system.

In planning its BRT system, **LAMATA benefited from the experiences of other BRT projects** in the developing world, especially the *Transmilenio* system in Bogotá, Colombia. As LAMATA's BRT services quickly became indispensable for Lagos residents, other cities—not only in Nigeria but elsewhere in Africa and beyond—increasingly asked for information and advice.

Meeting the demand for its learning meant that LAMATA would have to **strengthen its ability to manage knowledge for internal retention and replication and develop its capacity to disseminate what it had learned.** Following an in-depth assessment of its knowledge capacities, LAMATA management developed a vision statement: LAMATA will become "a foremost knowledge-sharing organization in the domestic and international transport sectors." Implementing that vision included the following key elements:

- A knowledge-sharing policy with clear roles and responsibilities for management and staff
- Incentive systems encouraging staff to share and collaborate
- An IT-based knowledge-management platform
- An online learning-management system for high-quality onboarding and staff training
- Methodologies to systematically and efficiently capture experiences as knowledge assets
- Tools and templates to make knowledge sharing more results-oriented

As a result, **LAMATA significantly improved its capacity to capture and apply its operational experiences** internally. The program has made LAMATA less vulnerable when key staff members leave and allows it to meet domestic and international requests for learning.

STEP 1: IDENTIFICATION

IDENTIFICATION

1.1 Why Is Identification Important?

The right knowledge at the right time and place can be crucial to overcoming barriers and aiding decision making. But what is the right knowledge? Organizations need to determine what is worth sharing and what is not—the "identification" step—ideally using clear criteria with which staff members can make that distinction. The process of identification involves targeting (such as identifying assets or gaps) and applying criteria for deciding on the importance of potential knowledge assets.

Identification at LAMATA

LAMATA management recognized that it was not easy to get staff to identify and capture mission-critical experiences by writing them down and submitting them to a central knowledge and learning team. So LAMATA specialists select experiences they believe will be most relevant for their colleagues to know about. At bimonthly team and department meetings they deliver short presentations, which are followed by a question and answer session, which tends to spark additional discussions and ideas. In this fashion, relevant experiences that might not have been noted or captured in real time are still identified. LAMATA's knowledge and learning team members document the meetings and transform the experiences and lessons learned into knowledge assets to be stored on the institutional knowledge-sharing platform.

Identification at Swachh Bharat Mission (SBM)

The government of India is encouraging the creation and identification of sanitation solutions, both by the public sector and by development partners. The key categories are technical remedies, behavioral and motivational innovations, and implementation solutions. The World Bank is institutionalizing organizational knowledge sharing at SBM to help officials carefully identify innovations and good practices that show results on the ground and are replicable. The solutions are being identified through an ongoing process of interaction and engagement with priority states and connecting the demand for knowledge to its supply. To accelerate the process, the government held a competition for multimedia documentation of sanitation solutions and results.

Identification at BNPB

BNPB has developed a scaled-up approach to identifying and capturing lessons learned about disaster management. At BNPB, a key criterion for selecting an experience is whether the lessons learned from it can be used by other disaster management professionals in the country. Trained knowledge-capturing teams document critical experiences and decision making—if possible, before and during as well as after a disaster. Focusing mainly on experiences related to local community involvement and advocacy with senior officials, the capturing teams identify a range of issues that they categorize according to discrete questions. These questions are the basis for organizing knowledge assets, which are uploaded onto BNPB's central knowledge library.

In addition, BNPB has instituted daily knowledge-sharing sessions in its headquarters in Jakarta. In three sessions every day, staff volunteer to share the latest findings or experiences from their field work, and each employee is mandated to share at least one experience every month. The sessions are critiqued by retired experts and recorded. Findings that are deemed important are uploaded as video-based knowledge assets to the central knowledge repository.

1.2 Identification Targets: Assets and Gaps

To identify critical knowledge (figure 1.1), organizations can focus on knowledge they are accumulating (assets) as well as on the knowledge they need (gaps). As explained below, the identification methods for the first approach are "continuous experience-based identification" and "comprehensive institution-wide identification." For the second approach, the process can address both group-wide gaps and individual needs.

Figure 1.1 Methods for Identifying Knowledge Assets and Gaps

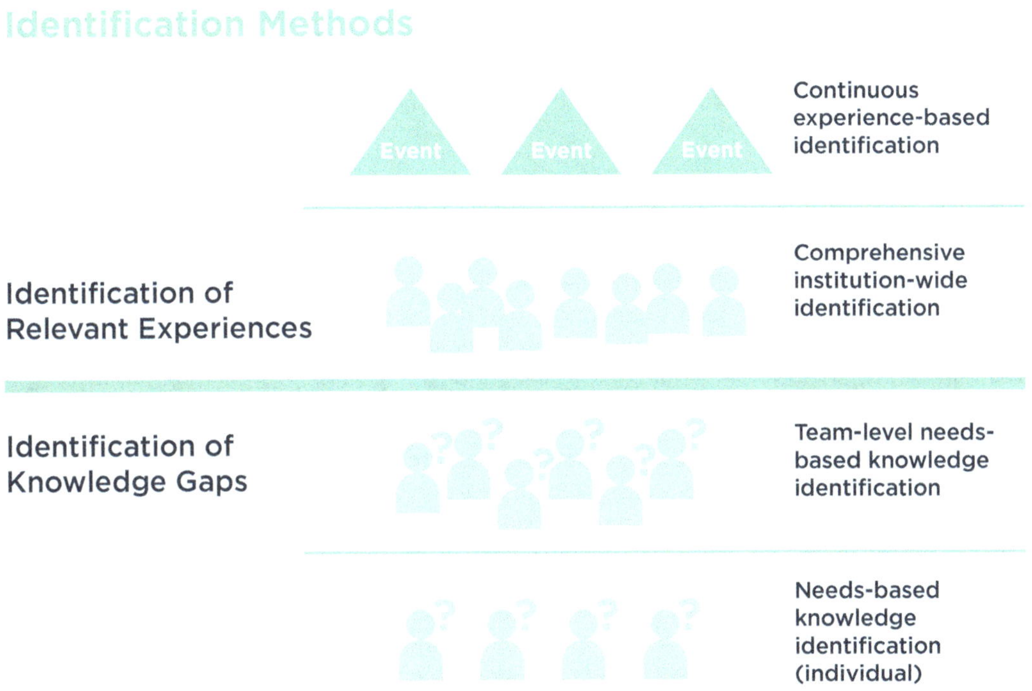

Identification Methods

Identification of Relevant Experiences
- Continuous experience-based identification
- Comprehensive institution-wide identification

Identification of Knowledge Gaps
- Team-level needs-based knowledge identification
- Needs-based knowledge identification (individual)

1.2.1 Continuous experience-based identification

This method is usually centered on events or activities that lead to high-value lessons learned. Some organizations may know which events qualify, while others may find it difficult to discern. But in each case, staff members make the selection, as they are the de facto experts involved.

Under this decentralized process, you may want to distribute to all staff members a "knowledge evaluation questionnaire" (as discussed further in section 1.4) to assess whether experiences and lessons learned are indeed critical. If so, they can proceed to use the well-known "5W-1H" questionnaire ("who, what, when, where, why, and how," section 1.4) to capture the basics. And as they use it, have them test whether their identified experiences and lessons learned are indeed critical by comparing them with their answers to the entries on the knowledge evaluation questionnaire.

When deciding on which experiences to capture, the goal must be to use limited knowledge- sharing resources efficiently and produce knowledge assets that will respond to your organization's most pressing needs.

However, *initial* identification cannot be time-consuming if it is to be continuous—few good ideas can survive a process that burdens someone's already full workload. Staff members may require incentives to perform even rapid continuous knowledge identification. The good news is that initial identification can be very quick. A staff member who notices something valuable can simply write down brief answers to the 5W-1H questionnaire, and others can later take things from there. This rapid identification should still be based on a strategic framework that has the above selection criteria at its heart.

1.2.2 Comprehensive institution-wide identification

Institution-wide identification systematically looks at all operations of the organization and identifies the knowledge assets in every department or business line. One way to do this is through a knowledge audit (discussed further below). With a knowledge audit, organizations will likely discover a wealth of know-how stemming from individual experiences that can be subsequently mined through capturing and packaging efforts. Comprehensive institution-wide identification of knowledge focuses mainly on identifying knowledge assets within an organization to meet concrete demand elsewhere in the organization or externally.

If your organization has a central knowledge management team that is tasked with identifying knowledge assets, the 5W-1H questionnaire can still be useful for individual interviews as well as for focus groups or in dedicated knowledge-sharing events.

1.2.3 Needs-based knowledge identification

Needs-based identification primarily revolves around surfacing knowledge gaps that must be filled if the organization is to operate effectively and sustainably. These gaps can include individuals' skill gaps, which can be overcome by targeted training; and comprehensive capacity gaps within units or departments. Each type can be assessed with a corresponding analysis employing tools discussed in section 1.4.

1.3 Criteria for Knowledge Capturing

It would be nice to capture and share all knowledge contained within your organization, but it is simply not feasible. Tough decisions must be made when deciding on which experiences to capture: the goal must be use limited knowledge-sharing resources efficiently and produce knowledge assets that will respond to your organization's most pressing needs.

A set of criteria helps practitioners decide whether to capture a particular lesson learned from an experience or event. Here are some of the most important to consider (figure 1.2):

1. Relevant—meets a demonstrable internal or external need
2. Narrowly focused
3. Shareable and replicable—artfully conveys insights or lessons learned so others can adapt and adopt
4. Easy to capture or record
5. Easy to validate
6. At risk of being lost

Let's look at these criteria in more detail, along with the need for measurable indicators.

Figure 1.2 Criteria for Determining Whether to Document an Experience

Relevance

In most cases, relevance will be the most important criterion. If an experience is not deemed useful for anybody, it will not warrant documenting. But what experiences are mission critical and which ones add just one more data point to an existing body of knowledge? It may be helpful to think of relevance as an initial filter. Will the organization and its staff or partners become better at what they are doing by replicating actions based on lessons learned from a given experience? If the answer is yes, the experience you plan to capture is likely mission-critical and worth documenting and sharing.

Focus

Perhaps the most challenging part of the identification process is getting the focus right. The future usability and accessibility of captured knowledge will largely depend on how well it is focused on a specific, concrete question. The broader the question underlying a knowledge asset, the less likely it will provide a useful answer. To avoid turning knowledge assets into full-fledged case studies (a common problem), regularly check whether the answers to the question are focused and practical. If a range of answers emerge, it might indicate that the knowledge asset should be broken up into smaller assets, each focused on a more specific question.

Shareability

Naturally the objective for capturing an experience is to share it with others for potential adaptation and replication. It is thus critical that experiences are indeed shareable. Capturing confidential information or politically charged information for the purpose of sharing may not be worth the effort. If the capturing and sharing of knowledge can possibly do more harm than good it may be better to refrain from it altogether and focus on those experiences for which there is an appreciative audience.

Easy to capture or record

Capturing experiences and lessons learned should be an achievable task. If critical stakeholders are impossible to locate and relevant background information can no longer be found, sound capturing of an experience without making too many assumptions may become difficult. It is therefore advisable to focus on those experiences for which sources can relatively easily be located.

Easy to validate

As we will discuss a bit later in this guide, validation is a critical part of the capturing process. It ensures high quality of the knowledge asset. Knowledge assets should be fairly easy to validate. If validators have no means to verify whether an experience actually took place as described, or the results claimed were actually achieved, the validity of the knowledge asset can become questionable.

Risk of getting lost

Last but not least it can be critical to capture experiences and lessons learned if they are at risk of getting lost. This can be the case when the primary experience holder retires or leaves the organization; or when a restructuring process causes significant changes in organizational structures and team compositions. In such cases it is advisable to document mission-critical knowledge to preserve it for those who need it.

1.3.1 A role for metrics

Establishing metrics for the use of knowledge assets can help in the later assessment of whether the assets met the expectations put forward in the identification phase. Here are some examples of measurable indicators:

» Number of practitioners that found the knowledge useful

» Number of practitioners that used the knowledge to solve challenges in their own context

» Number of practitioners that had follow-up questions on the knowledge asset for further clarification or elaboration

» Number of practitioners that were able to access the knowledge asset

» Number of practitioners that recommended the knowledge asset to other peers

» Percentage of targeted practitioners that are using the suggested process or recommendations in the knowledge asset

Build each knowledge asset on a very specific question. Unlike a case study, a knowledge asset should provide guidance on resolving a distinct problem. Take, for example, the following two questions that have been identified as challenges to be captured:

(1) What can be done to build disaster emergency shelters in local communities?

(2) How can local government officials persuade resisting local communities to build disaster emergency shelters on ancestral land?

The first question could relate to many issues, such as type of construction, who will build the shelter, financing, planning, etc. Each of the above may be best addressed with another specific question that provides a distinct answer. Indeed, many seemingly distinct knowledge assets can be split, each focused on a more narrowly focused question. The second question represents that narrower focus; it allows for a much more targeted answer, ultimately being much more useful for a local government official faced with that specific problem.

1.4 Useful Tools and Templates for Identifying Relevant Knowledge

1.4.1 Knowledge evaluation questionnaire

"Does it matter?" may be the key question to ask when identifying operational experiences and lessons learned. To make sure that it does matter, and to whom, use a questionnaire that can be checked off before taking any further action (see appendix A.1 for a sample). As noted above, when time is of the essence, this assessment can come after a rapid execution of the 5W-1H questionnaire.

1.4.2 5W-1H knowledge identification questionnaire

This easy to understand and popular method for identifying knowledge that should be captured and retained asks the questions "who, what, where, when, why, and how?" The questionnaire systematically and consistently anchors experiences and lessons learned with the essential data used in answering the questions. Knowledge and learning staff can use the form to survey colleagues within the organization for important experiential knowledge, which can be refined in subsequent steps (see appendix A.2 for a sample 5W-1H questionnaire).

Figure 1.3 Elements of the 5W-1H Questionnaire

1.4.3 Peer-assisted learning

Peer-assisted learning (PAL) is a simple, easy-to-implement intervention in which one team calls a meeting or workshop to seek knowledge and insights from other people within your organization. This formal appeal to peers serves as a rapid, cross-organizational survey of related knowledge as well as an opportunity to brainstorm and co-create new instructional content. The objective is to cast a wide net for relevant but often undocumented experiences and draw together a set of solutions from a diverse group of colleagues.

PAL interventions can take as little as an hour, depending on the scope of the task. They should include a facilitator not involved with the project at hand who can provide a neutral, synthesizing perspective, and appeal to the group's collective experience for specific task- or process-oriented insights. Documenting a PAL intervention also affords an opportunity to capture the results for future use.

1.4.4 Social network analysis

In contrast to an organization chart that shows formal reporting relationships, a social network analysis chart shows informal relationships: From whom do people seek information and knowledge? With whom do they share their information and knowledge? It allows managers to visualize and understand the many relationships and informal institutional structures that can facilitate or impede knowledge creation and sharing.

Social network analysis has significant strategic value. First, understanding your organization's underlying knowledge flows allows you to locate informal knowledge resources. Second, it can facilitate validation of those resources. And third, it can support monitoring and evaluation in later phases of the knowledge process.

1.4.5 Knowledge audit

A knowledge audit allows organizations to take a comprehensive approach to identifying important lessons and takeaways held by their staff. The audit typically also documents who "owns" the existing knowledge, how it is created, where it is located, how it flows between staff or other key stakeholders, and how it is used. A knowledge audit usually relies on a combination of methods, including online surveys, focus-group discussions, stakeholder interviews, and process or content analysis (see appendix A.3 for a sample knowledge audit survey).

1.4.6 Organizational knowledge gap analysis

While a knowledge audit looks at what is available in the organization, a knowledge gap analysis identifies what an organization is missing—that is, the difference between what an organization should know and what it actually does know. The analysis can help prioritize areas where knowledge needs to be gained and shared. As the organization evolves, requirements for new business or service areas can be added to the analysis to help the organization develop the emerging mix of required skills (see appendix A.4 for a sample template of an organizational knowledge gap analysis).

1.4.7 Individual skills gap analysis

Valuable knowledge may reside in the heads of a few key employees. While these employees are therefore critically important, they are for the same reason the Achilles heel of the organization. When they move on, they take a wealth of knowledge with them that can be hard to reproduce or find elsewhere. An "individual skills gap" analysis can help avoid such loss, as it can map who has critical knowledge and who needs to learn it. The process can also serve to develop personal learning plans and growth perspectives or to prepare staff in a timely way for emerging or changing job descriptions (see appendix A.5 for a sample template of an individual skills gap analysis).

1.5 The Output

By assembling some or all of the above tools for knowledge identification, you will have a framework for determining whether a particular experience is worth capturing and sharing. If the answer is yes, proceed to step 2: capturing. If the answer is no, stop there.

For organizations interested in identifying skills gaps, the output is slightly different. A thorough skills gap analysis will usually provide valuable insights into areas that merit investment in learning and skills building.

1.6 Checklist for Designing the Identification Step

Question	Yes
Are we clear about the identification intervals (continuous or needs-based)?	
If the approach is needs-based, are we clear about the skills gaps we are trying to address?	
Are we clear where experiences and solutions can come from?	
Have we tasked specific stakeholders with identifying solutions?	
Have we developed identification criteria to sharpen the focus and limit the scope of subsequent capturing tasks?	

STEP 2: CAPTURING

CAPTURING

2.1 Why Is Capturing Important?

Once you have determined that an experience or lesson learned is valuable to others and worth documenting, you are ready to start capturing. Capturing is the process of converting the knowledge that resides in people's heads into tangible, explicit knowledge assets. This usually involves recording it in a format that can be stored, further processed, adapted, and shared. Common media formats to capture experiences and lessons learned include text, audio, video, images, and graphics. Making experiential knowledge explicit helps to surface the often hidden knowledge in an organization. Without capturing for accessibility, the knowledge that resides in an individual's head cannot be easily distributed within the organization or with external partners. Capturing is the critical action that leads to creation of a library of knowledge assets that can be shared regardless of the availability of one individual.

Overcoming the phenomenon of sticky knowledge. It is noteworthy that knowledge can be quite "sticky." In other words it can be difficult to capture and share it due to lack of an organizational knowledge sharing culture or lack of willingness of individuals to share. A knowledge-capturing effort cannot be forced upon people. It should go hand-in-hand with a wider culture change effort in an organization based on participatory discussion processes, senior management support and role modeling, and adequate incentives. More on the development of an organizational knowledge sharing culture can be found in the World Bank's handbook on "Becoming a Knowledge Sharing Organization."

Capturing at BNPB

To efficiently document the vast amount of knowledge generated by more than 400 district-level disaster management agencies, the Indonesian Disaster Management Authority (BNPB) has developed internal and external mechanisms for knowledge capturing. Internally, BNPB is organizing daily knowledge-sharing sessions in their headquarters, during which the staff can share experiences and lessons learned. Further, each employee is mandated to share an experience at these sessions at least once a month. The sharing sessions are captured and edited to feed a central knowledge repository.

Externally, BNPB has started to partner with academic institutions to capture lessons learned. Capturing teams, mainly consisting of current or former students of disaster management graduate programs in Indonesia, are trained by faculty at local universities to conduct targeted interviews with key stakeholders involved in disaster response activities. These interviews occur either during or shortly after a disaster event to ensure recollections of decisions and their effects are fresh in the minds of the stakeholders. The captured knowledge is collected and compiled into knowledge assets using standardized templates including text and video. Through this effort, BNPB is building a pool of local emergency response experiences that can inform future events in a just-in-time manner.

Through its training center, BNPB is also using captured knowledge in structured learning materials for systematically training local disaster management agencies on effective strategies and actions.

Capturing at Swachh Bharat Mission (SBM)

As it looks for ways to stop open defecation in India, SBM captures successful local initiatives in various languages, largely using video, presentations, and PDF or text documents. SBM began its capturing program by delivering hands-on training in the use of video to more than 200 sanitation officials from three states (Haryana, Rajasthan, and Uttar Pradesh) to regularly identify, capture, validate, and package local sanitation solutions. In groups of up to 50 over three days, the participants learned to interview local stakeholders, using their own smartphones to capture and edit video clips. While not of TV broadcast quality, the smartphone videos provide an immediate and vivid way to showcase local innovations through the words of local community members providing tips and recommendations to peers. In addition, a select group of the trainees have become trainers themselves in capturing local solutions through video.

2.2 Telling the Story: Logically Organizing the Important Elements

Organizations may choose different approaches to capturing, but they will always have to think about what they capture and how they capture. We start here with the "what" and then discuss the various techniques for capturing.

Although you may not know what a specific experience entails before you begin capturing it, the capturing process should follow a logical structure that records information in a way that can be used later to create a knowledge asset. We suggest that you use a simple storyline structure to organize your thoughts about the experience as well as to organize the structure of the knowledge asset you will later create out of the captured material (figure 2.1).

Figure 2.1 Storyline for Capturing and Structuring a Knowledge Asset

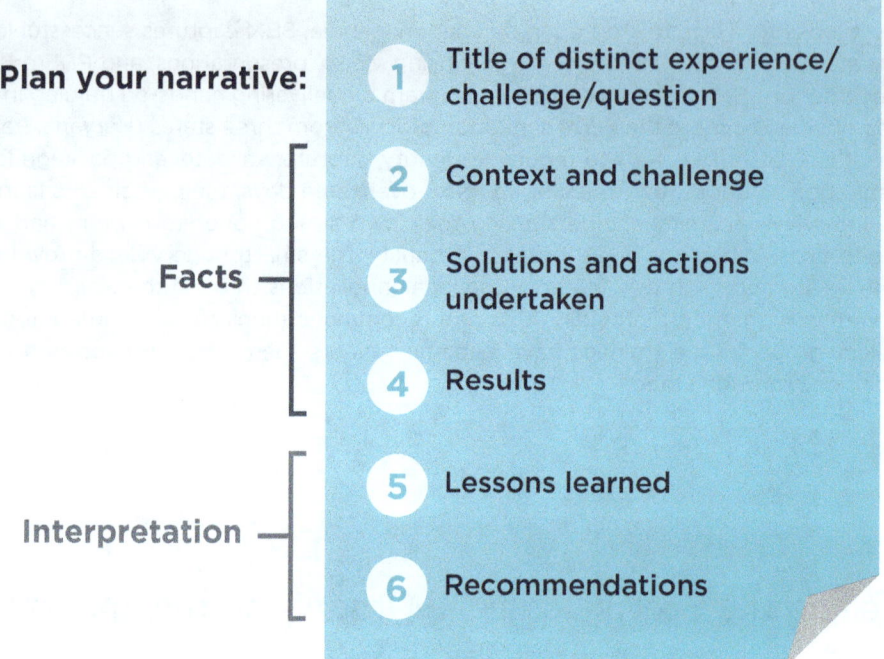

Making experiential knowledge explicit helps to surface the often hidden knowledge in an organization.... Capturing is the critical action that allows knowledge assets to be shared regardless of the availability of one individual.

Stories usually have a beginning, middle, and end, and so will the story you are about to document. It starts with a compelling title that suggests what to expect in the story. The beginning of the story itself will focus on the context and challenge of a particular experience. You will then move on to the description of the actions taken to overcome the challenge, highlight the results, and close with concrete lessons learned and transferrable recommendations.

The more closely you follow this structure in your capturing process, the easier it will be to turn the raw material you have recorded into a knowledge asset from which others can learn.

Let's look at the elements of this storyline in more detail, including the questions that should be asked to help ensure it has the necessary detail and scope (these questions are collected in figure 2.2).

Also use the guiding questions in figure 2.2 when formatting your knowledge asset (in step 4). They will help you test whether your knowledge asset provides sufficient detail to answer a recipient's demand for learning from a given experience.

2.2.1 The title

A succinct, clear, and compelling title suggests what will be in the story and draws the reader in. At some point, the story will become one of many knowledge assets, so it is important to be as specific as possible to provide a good idea of what specific solution to what specific problem can be found in the resulting knowledge asset. The title may be revised later on to make it more concrete once the content is more fully developed.

A good starting point for the title may be the specific question you have identified by applying the guidelines in the previous chapter. An example of a good title (using the case of disaster management in Indonesia) would be: "How to ensure post-disaster livelihoods by using cattle evacuation and upfront engagement with community leaders." That title lets the reader know what to expect. It provides a brief description of the problem (ensuring livelihoods after disasters) and the solution (upfront engagement with community leaders in the affected area to discuss cattle evacuation). A less informative title would be "Evacuating cattle from Mount Sinabung." Here it is not clear what the problem is, nor does the headline give an indication of the solution.

Put the specific question, problem, or challenge in the title. A common mistake in titles, and in knowledge assets altogether, is to make them generic. The more concrete and closely defined a challenge is, including via the title, the more likely the captured information will be seen and used by others. Generalities and vague ideas will not help development practitioners who are grappling with a specific challenge and are searching for concrete solutions. The title is the way to get their attention.

If you choose a title at the outset, go back to after you have completed the knowledge asset to see whether the two still match. In particular, if the content of the knowledge asset is broader than the title, you may need to split up the content into several knowledge assets that focus on a more specific challenge, each with its own more specific title.

Questions to verify whether the title works:

- » Will someone who has not yet gone through the knowledge asset know what it is about?
- » Would the title also work for other stories? If so, it may be too generic.

2.2.2 Context

Background information can be critical to evaluate the transferability of an experience to another context. Every experience is rooted in its own circumstances that will likely significantly affect its potential solution paths.. Hence, this section should give enough detail to judge transferability by providing relevant information on location, the key actors, special circumstances and, where applicable, the sociopolitical and historical background.

Questions to answer for the context section:

- » What is the background of the challenge or problem?
- » What was the actual challenge or problem?
- » What caused this challenge or problem to arise?
- » What were its implications or consequences?
- » Where and when did the event or experience take place?
- » What was the situation before the event?
- » Who was involved? Who was affected?

2.2.3 Actions taken

A careful description of what actually happened—the experience itself—will show how those involved dealt with the challenge or problem. Be sure to outline the solution paths and, where applicable, any options available to the decision makers. Also provide the reasons that a specific solution was chosen. It may also be useful to discuss potential barriers that arose during implementation of the solution and how they were addressed. Remember, the recipients of the knowledge asset will not have been part of the experience: make sure you provide enough detail so others can fully understand, adapt, and replicate the solution path.

Questions to answer for the actions taken section:

- » What actions were taken to overcome the challenge or problem?
- » Who was involved in the actions and in what role?
- » What was the sequence of the activities en route to the solution?
- » Why where certain decisions made?
- » Were mistakes made and, if so, what were they?
- » Were barriers to implementing the solution encountered and, if so, how were they overcome?

2.2.4 Results

Your audience will want to know what changed after an event. Create an outline showing whether the actions taken had positive or negative effects. Your description must be detailed as well as concise. If possible, quantify a certain result and measure it against a baseline. This information will provide credibility for the approach and will help readers make informed choices on use of the knowledge asset for replication.

Questions to answer for the results section:

- » What were the results of the actions taken?
- » Are these results fully attributable to the actions taken? To what extent did other elements influence the result?
- » Which key activities ultimately led to which positive or negative results?
- » Were there any additional positive or negative results worth mentioning?
- » How did the various stakeholders react to the activities? Why?

2.2.5 Lessons learned

Perhaps the most important element of the knowledge asset is the account of lessons learned. Here you will describe the key takeaways from the experience—what the expert would want recipients of the knowledge asset to remember. Unlike the results section, the emphasis here is on using simple terms to describe a few major points that synthesize the learning from the experience. Nonetheless, as in the previous sections, specificity is critical. Avoid generalities such as "community involvement is important," "adequate communication is critical," or "timing is essential." A good takeaway may have several parts and may be presented in bullet points. For example: "On two occasions, we engaged with community leaders and women's groups in three-hour facilitated focus group sessions that each brought together 25 to 40 community members. The sessions helped us to collect expectations, address concerns at an early stage, and build trust."

Questions to answer for the lessons learned section:

- » What were the most important lessons learned from the experience?
- » What would you do differently? What would you do in the same way?
- » How did these lessons affect the success or failure of the actions?
- » Whose involvement was important and why?

2.2.6 Recommendations

The purpose of the knowledge asset is to help others who may face similar challenges, so in this section the expert considers what the lessons learned in the previous section may mean for others. In doing so, the expert may have to sift out details unique to the original situation to focus on aspects that are more widely applicable. But again, the advice should be rooted in the experience, so avoid generalities. For example, if the involvement of stakeholders is important, a recommendation such as "always involve all stakeholders early on" simply does not provide enough detail for action. Rather, explain which types of stakeholders, why, when, and how. You can also present these recommendations in bullet points. For instance, a set of such points may be introduced as follows: "When resettling small cattle-raising communities away from volcano-affected areas, insuring the sustainability of livelihoods is critical and may best be achieved by including a relocation plan for the cattle. These plans are best co-developed with the local community early on to build strong buy-in. A sound plan will include the following elements where applicable: . . . "

Questions to solicit input for the recommendations section:

- What are the most important conclusions and recommendations from the experience?
- What would you recommend others to do when facing similar challenges?
- What aspects merit particular attention and how?
- What would you avoid?

Figure 2.2 Questions to Ensure You Have Compiled a Useful and Complete Storyline

1. **Title**
   » Will someone who has not yet gone through the knowledge asset know what it is about?
   » Would the title also work for other stories? If so, it may be too generic.

2. **Context**
   » What is the background of the challenge or problem?
   » What was the actual challenge or problem?
   » What caused this challenge or problem to arise?
   » What were its implications or consequences?
   » Where and when did the event or experience take place?
   » What was the situation before the event?
   » Who was involved? Who was affected?

3. **Actions taken**
   » What actions were taken to overcome the challenge or problem?
   » Who was involved in the actions and in what role?
   » What was the sequence of the activities en route to the solution?

- » Why where certain decisions made?
- » Were mistakes made and, if so, what were they?
- » Were barriers to implementing the solution encountered and, if so, how were they overcome?
- » What resources were used to make it happen?

4. **Results**
- » What were the results of the actions taken?
- » Are these results fully attributable to the actions taken? To what extent did other elements influence the result?
- » Which key activities ultimately led to which positive or negative results?
- » Were there any additional positive or negative results worth mentioning?
- » How did the various stakeholders react to the activities? Why?

5. **Lessons learned**
- » What were the most important lessons learned from the experience?
- » What would you do differently? What would you do in the same way?
- » How did these lessons affect the success or failure of the actions?
- » Whose involvement was important and why?

6. **Recommendations**
- » What are the most important conclusions and recommendations from the experience?
- » What would you recommend others to do when facing similar challenges?
- » What aspects merit particular attention and how?
- » What would you avoid?

2.3 Techniques for Systematically Capturing Experiences and Lessons Learned

A given capturing methodology cannot be applied to all organizations—every workplace must adapt its capturing strategy to its specific context and business needs. The main question is, who will be responsible for capturing? A menu of options exists (figure 2.3). Small organizations with few staff members may choose to build a dedicated capturing team with knowledge management and communications officers who frequently interview colleagues on important lessons learned. This approach is useful where broader staff readiness in terms of skills and incentives for capturing is low.

In contrast, large organizations with geographically dispersed activities may need an external partner to help with knowledge capturing. Even so, many large institutions, especially in the private sector, provide incentives for their staff to continuously capture and share knowledge that is critical for business. If a strong knowledge-sharing culture exists, such decentralized capturing and sharing is probably the most successful approach, although it requires strong systems for unified content formatting, rapid storage, and sharing to yield the desired results. However, self-capturing by staff also has a risk. Capturing of our own actions introduces a significant bias. We make assumptions, tell the story from our own - subjective - perspective. In such cases it will be important to have strong and more neutral validation mechanisms in place.

Figure 2.3 Determinants of Alternative Approaches to Capturing

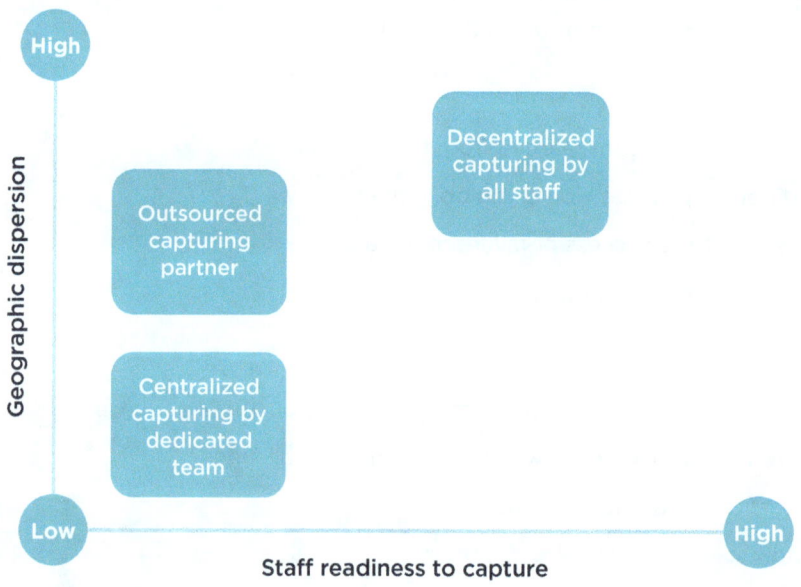

Once leaders have decided on who will be in charge of capturing, the technical skills and steps for capturing will vary little across organizations: (1) solid preparation and (2) a good sense of various capturing activities, all of which are most effective if they are driven by a journalistic mindset that creates takeaways that are meaningful to third parties.

2.3.1 Preparation for knowledge capturing

Sound preparation is required for all logistical matters of knowledge-capturing activities. Contact the expert knowledge stakeholders in advance and clearly define the time and location for the capturing activity.

What is a good time to capture knowledge? The answer is simple and definite: as soon as possible! The more time that passes after an event or experience, the more likely that important details will be forgotten (figure 2.4). Retention rates drops dramatically in the first days following an event or exposure to new knowledge. After one day, 60 percent of the new information is already forgotten, and after five days a person typically remembers only one-fourth of the information. The rate of recollection remains relatively stable beyond five days.

Figure 2.4 The Forgetting Curve

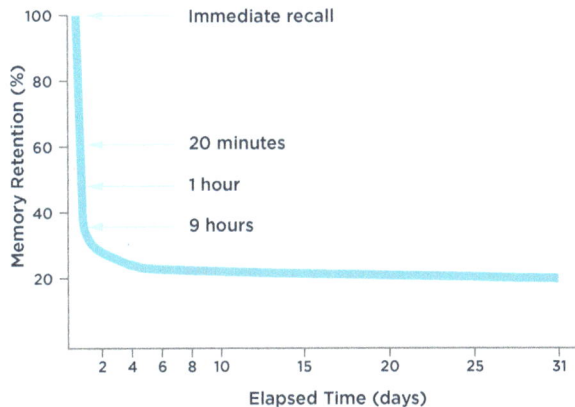

Source: Stephen M. Stahl, Richard L. Davis, Dennis H. Kim, Nicole Gellings Lowe, Richard E. Carlson Jr., Karen Fountain, and Meghan M. Grady, 2010, "Play it Again: The Master Psychopharmacology Program as an Example of Interval Learning in Bite-Sized Portions," *CNS Spectrums* 15 (8): 491–504.

Capturers will not need to be subject-matter experts, but they should have a basic understanding of the substance to be covered as well as a good overall picture of the experience. If the experience has been identified through a formal process, as outlined in Step 1 (Chapter 1), the capturers can review documents such as the 5W-1H knowledge identification questionnaire (appendix A.2). They may also gather reports, articles, pictures, video footage, and references to other stakeholders who can possibly provide insights on the experience.

Plan ahead and be prepared. Before you start capturing, make sure you have everything in place. The following checklist can help you evaluate your plan:

» Is your plan feasible?
» Do you have the right resources (manpower, tools) to execute the plan?
» Are the experts available?
» Are the experts well selected? Are you missing anyone?
» Are there potential risks that are not covered?
» Is your plan likely to address the key questions raised in your challenge?
» Are the chosen methods appropriate to adequately capture the experience?
» Is the chosen technique appropriate to optimally showcase the content?

But! Sometimes opportunities arise that may not come again! In such cases, capturing must happen on the fly, despite the lack of time for preparation. Once recorded or documented in some fashion, the information can always be edited, enhanced, or expanded.

2.3.2 Capturing activities

Experiential knowledge and lessons learned can be captured with a variety of methods. Selecting the methods will depend on organizational policies, the availability of technology and support tools, personal preferences, and the capturer's skill set.

We distinguish between two types of activities for capturing operational experiences and lessons learned: those conducted by an individual and those conducted collaboratively (figure 2.5). While capturing activities can be conducted in person, they are increasingly taking place online. Some activities, such as collaborative workspaces and wikis, combine capturing with knowledge sharing so that knowledge is documented and shared at the same time.

Some activities require more skill and preparation than others (table 2.1). But they all can provide the grist for the compilation of knowledge assets offering a story of important takeaways and lessons learned from past or current experiences and projects.

Figure 2.5 Individual and Collaborative Types of Capturing Activities

Individual	Collaborative
Interview	After-action review
Storytelling	Focus group
Observation	Wiki
Blog	Collaborative workspace
Back-to-office report	Webinar
	Online forum
	Community of practice (CoP)
	Premortem review

Here are short explanations of the activities listed in figure 2.5 and table 2.1. Further details on all (except for the back-to-office report and premortem review), in some cases including a discussion of advantages and disadvantages, are in appendix B. A key tool for many of the capturing processes discussed here is a video recorder (whether in a smartphone or as a separate camera). See appendix C for details on how to make the most effective use of this tool.

Individual activities

Interview

The most direct way to find out what someone knows is to ask, so it is not surprising that interviewing is the most frequently used knowledge-capturing approach. The interviewer asks questions to elicit facts, experiences, or reflections from one or more interviewees. Interviews can be captured on paper, with a voice recorder, or with a video camera. Usually conducted in person, interviews can also be carried out by telephone or videoconference.

Storytelling

This activity is the most directly adaptable to the storyline structure of a knowledge asset. Storytelling increases the potential for meaningful knowledge capturing and sharing through its narrative structure. Storytelling can supplement analytical thinking and is thus a good way to exchange information and generate understanding. Through telling the whole story of an experience, the expert will often start to realize the value and relevance of the unique experience. Key messages are often easier to understand and remember when presented in a story. Many of the other capturing methods discussed here are venues for storytelling combined with opportunities for others to augment the story with further ideas, documentation, and refinement.

Observation

Knowledge elicitation often begins with someone's observation of a task performed by the expert. Observation provides a first idea of an interesting experience. This may be the case when watching somebody else plan and conduct a multistakeholder conversation or witnessing the process of policy development on a given topic. Observations ideally occur in the expert's working environment, thereby providing insight into actual behavior. However, not all relevant experiences can be observed in their natural surroundings (for example accidents or unexpected events). Observation methodologies vary depending on the subject of the observation, the role of the observer (participatory or passive), and the method of recording (writing, photos, audio, video).

Blog

A blog (short for web log) is a frequently updated website presenting the written opinions and experiences (often also with audio and video) of an individual or group along with readers' comments. It may be public or restricted to members of a community. A blog enables groups of people to discuss areas of interest, review different opinions, and gain new information. It can encourage dissemination of operational experiences and lessons learned through storytelling.

Back-to-office report

The back-to-office report is usually a brief synopsis of the purpose, experiences, and lessons learned from visits to clients, peer organizations, conferences, or other out-of-office events. Capturing key takeaways allows those who didn't participate to learn from colleagues' experiences outside the organization.

Collaborative activities

After-action review

Occurring during or immediately after an operation or event, an after-action review captures the lessons learned from successes and failures using a specific process. It is an opportunity for a team to reflect on an event or an activity so that they can do better the next time. The after-action review facilitates continuous assessment of organizational performance, ensuring that learning takes place.

Focus group

A focus group is a set of individuals selected for their experiences or opinions regarding an action or ongoing activity. With a set of guiding questions posed by a moderator, a group discussion can provide a great deal of information and many insights. The group setting allows participants to respond to and build on each other's comments.

Wiki

A wiki is a website that that anyone with access to the Internet and with the appropriate access rights can edit. Wikis allow users to format text, add images and media, and create links between pages. Wiki users do not need to know how to program to create content on the web. Wikis give users the ability to work collaboratively on the same document or collection of documents. The only software needed is an Internet browser. Wikis can be used for a variety of purposes but are especially suitable for capturing, editing, and sharing operational experiences and lessons learned regardless of geographic location.

Collaborative workspace

Collaborative workspace, also called shared workspace or groupware, is a broad term for various types of web-based environments in which users can interact with each other independently of time and location. Collaborative workspace users can document and share operational experiences through text, images, and videos. Once documents are uploaded, user can interact with each other through comments, annotations, and discussion threads.

Webinar

Webinars (short for web-based seminars) support discussions, presentations, lectures, and training events, allowing participants to share a combination of video, audio, text, and presentations regardless of their physical location. Although active participants must be online at the same time, webinars can be recorded for later online learning by others.

Online forum

An online forum, also sometimes referred to as a message board or electronic billboard, is a website in which a community can engage in online discussions. Users post messages on the site for others to read and respond to. The messages are often organized and archived in threaded discussions around a specific subject. Often, a forum administrator or editors review the messages for suitability before they are posted. Unlike conferencing tools, which are synchronous (employed in real time), forums are asynchronous—people can participate when they choose. Forums are therefore particularly useful when participants are spread across many time zones.

Community of practice (CoP)

A web-based community of practice organizes experts in a specific domain of interest to engage in a process of collective learning. To support knowledge creation and sharing, the CoP should be structured around specific learning goals. Effective CoPs often rely on a combination of instruction-based and group-based learning activities conducted in person or via chat, forum, discussion, or conferencing, sometimes along with audio and video.

A special case: Premortem review

In a medical setting, a postmortem allows health professionals and the family to learn what caused a patient's death—to the benefit of everyone but the patient. A premortem review is the opposite of a postmortem. It is designed to fortify a project from the outset by asking team members to consider how and why the project may fail. But rather than brainstorm potential mishaps, the premortem participants imagine that the worst has already happened—that the project has failed spectacularly. The question is, why? Participants independently (and usually anonymously) write down every reason they can think of for the failure, including those that might normally go unmentioned in the interest of politeness; they then are encouraged to collectively imagine solutions to this array of hypothetical failures.

Table 2.1 Features of Selected Knowledge-Capturing Activities and Resources

Activity or Resource	Users		Dynamics		Adoption and Operation			ICT	Preparation		Supported Media			
	Individual	Group	Simple events/actions	Continuous process	Easy	Moderate	Difficult	Requires ICT support	Short set-up time	Long set-up time	Text	Audio	Images	Video
After-action Review		●	●	○	●				●		●		●	○
Back-to-office Report	●		●		●				●		●		●	○
Blog	●	○	●			●		●	●		●		●	
Collaborative Workspace		●	●				●	●	●		●	●	●	●
Community of Practice		●	●				●	●	●		●	●	●	●
Focus Group		●	●		●				●		●	○		○
Online Forum		●	●		●			●	●		●			
Interview	●	○	●		●				●		●	●		●
Observation	○		●	○	●				●		○	●	●	●
Premartem Review		●	●	○	●				●					
Storytelling	●		●	○	●				●		●	●		
Wiki	●	●	●				●	●	●		●	●	●	●

● frequently used
○ sometimes used
ICT = information and communication technology

2.4 The Output

The output of the capturing process is a knowledge asset consisting of some or all of the following elements: video, audio, graphics, and text (see appendix D for examples). The knowledge asset you compile from the capturing phase should tell a compelling and complete story that is ready for the next step: validation by peers or superiors.

You may have recorded interviews or focus group sessions. If you followed the storyline outlined above, the recordings (whether audio alone or video) will often already be in the sequence in which they will appear in the knowledge asset. Nonetheless, you may have to shorten these recordings to convey the story with the optimal amount of information.

2.5 Checklist for Designing the Capturing Step

Question	Yes
Are we clear about the target audience for the knowledge we are capturing?	
Are we clear who is capturing experiences and lessons learned and are they appropriately trained?	
Are we ensuring that experiences are captured in a timely manner?	
Have we selected the appropriate capturing activity?	
Have we provided guidance for the logistical set-up of capturing activities?	
Have we selected the appropriate capturing media?	
Are we clear about which language(s) should be used for the captured experience?	
Are we following a clear set of templates for the capturing of experiences and lessons learned?	
Are we including contextual information to appropriately situate the experience?	
Are we ensuring knowledge capturers are providing enough how-to detail and helpful lessons learned so captured solutions can potentially be replicated?	
Are we sure there is evidence for the documented results?	

STEP 3: VALIDATION

VALIDATION

3.1 Why Is Validation Important?

Experiential knowledge is based on a person's recollection of events and of experiences related to those events. Personal perception is naturally subjective and influenced by underlying assumptions. So, when capturing experiences, the information is likely to be more reliable if it comes from a variety of perspectives. Another key process to ensure that the knowledge asset is as useful as possible—and to avoid the production of misleading assets—is to have its accuracy, relevance, and usefulness *validated* by one or more experts. Validation is the quality-control part of the program that produces knowledge assets. Only accurate, relevant, concise, and useful knowledge assets should enter an organization's knowledge management system, and a process must be established to uphold those standards.

Validation at Swachh Bharat Mission (SBM)

At India's SBM, captured knowledge resources are validated at three levels. The first validation happens during identification and capture, usually by the capturing team. This team will self-review to ensure that the knowledge is relevant, innovative, truly good practice, accurate, technically sound, and sharable. The focus of capturing is on "how-to" and "experiential learning," and capturing teams use a check-list for self-validation.

> continued

> continued from the previous page

The second validation is undertaken by the magistrates for each district, who are tasked with validating relevance, accuracy, and potential reputational risk and then uploading the knowledge assets to the central repository. The magistrates may be supported by a dedicated validation team, which may include technical experts in sanitation.

Lastly, SBM mission directors in the state will validate. State government can invite technical experts, Rapid Action Learning Units (small teams set up in some states to advise decision makers on implementation problems), and the state's knowledge-management experts to peer review the knowledge resources. Beyond these three levels, the national ministry will also periodically undertake random validation of the knowledge resources to ensure quality.

Validation at BNPB

The Indonesian Disaster Management Authority (BNPB) instituted a formal review and validation mechanism to ensure that the growing number of knowledge assets recorded by capturing teams across the country undergo a thorough quality check before being formatted and shared widely. BNPB's Knowledge Management Task Force consists of director-level and expert-level staff members from various operational departments as well as the head of BNPB's training center, and it is headed by a member of senior management. The committee regularly reviews drafts of draft knowledge assets, often referring questions, substantive comments, or suggestions for further improvement to the authors. After committee approval, the asset is posted to a central knowledge repository for further dissemination and sharing.

3.2 Validation Criteria

Choosing the criteria for evaluating knowledge assets is fundamental to the validation process. Organizations must carefully select and refine the criteria and rank them by importance. A few common evaluation standards for knowledge assets are listed below (and as a checklist in table 3.1).

» Does the operational experience or lesson learned add to what is already known as a practice that yields successful outcomes? Is it a valuable contribution to the operational practice of the organization?

» Does the knowledge asset address a distinct issue or challenge?

» Is the content correct?

- » Is it presented clearly, so that it cannot be misinterpreted?
- » Is the formal presentation and formatting of the content adequate?
- » Is the language clear and appropriate?
- » Is enough context provided for understanding the particular circumstances in which the operational experience occurred?
- » Are concrete lessons and recommendations included?
- » Does the knowledge asset create any risk, including reputational or regarding use of intellectual property?

3.3 Variations in Validation Structures

A validation process should be established early in the planning of the overall knowledge-sharing program. The structure chosen for the validation process is likely to evolve along with the larger program because validation isn't a single process; it can happen in different ways, ranging from a rigorous formal review process with one or several sign-off stages to informal feedback by a peer. These variations can be captured in a matrix of six organizational structures for conducting validation (figure 3.1). They vary according to their degree of formality and outside support.

Figure 3.1 Six Organizational Structures for Validation

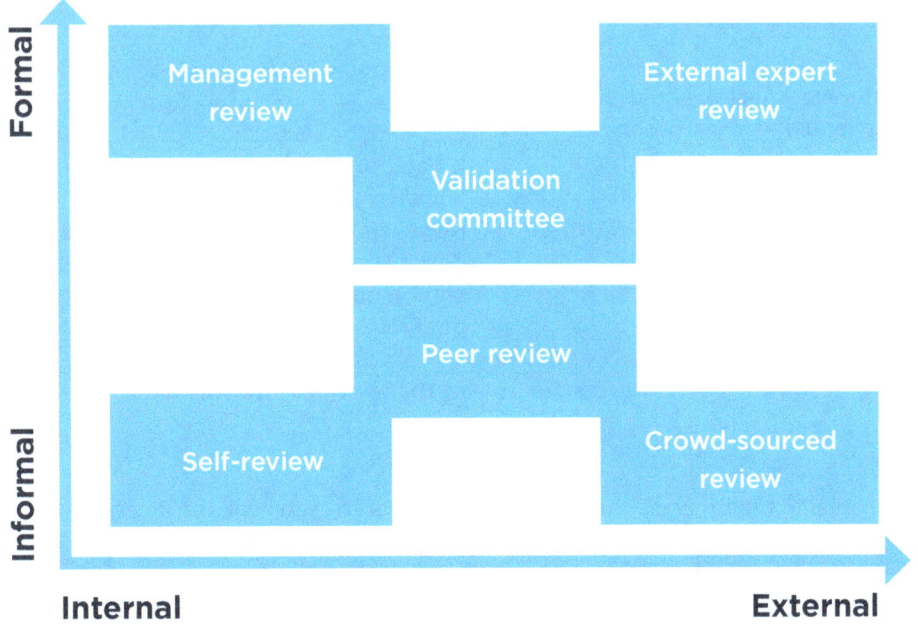

3.3.1 Self-review

In the lightest form of validation, the author of the knowledge asset can decide whether it is acceptable. Some institutions, such as organizations of trusted experts or those with a high degree of collaboration, allow authors to submit a knowledge asset *without* formal validation. Authors can be staff members or part of management at any level of the organization, or they may be people tasked with the development of knowledge assets. Self-review speeds the process of generating knowledge assets, but it offers no defense against any lack of objectivity on the part of the author.

3.3.2 Management review

Depending on the organization's size and management's availability, a review by the leadership may accelerate or slow down the process of knowledge capturing. In the best-case scenario, management assesses the content with little delay. Even then, however, management may not be adequately qualified to review a very technical knowledge asset. But because management is ultimately responsible for the knowledge assets, they should be involved at least when the knowledge-capturing program is being designed. Doing so will send an important signal that management values quality assurance in knowledge capturing.

3.3.3 Validation committee

A committee responsible for validation can be useful whether or not management is directly involved in the process. Typically made up of experts from various departments in the organization, the committee can also include experts in the field of knowledge management or learning to give additional insight into the suitability of the assets for learning activities.

3.3.4 Peer review

Only accurate, relevant, concise, and useful knowledge assets should enter an organization's knowledge management system, and a process must be established to uphold those standards.

Review by colleagues, usually from within the organization, is a common form of validation. Peers can include experts involved in the experience, co-authors, client-users, and disseminators of the knowledge asset. In some cases, involving neutral reviewers who do not have a stake in the domain of the knowledge asset can be helpful. Peer review can be quick and cost-effective, although external peer review can take longer than internal review. In organizational cultures that interpret negative comments as hostility, peer review may not be suitable until critiquing becomes generally accepted as part of the organizational culture.

3.3.5 External expert review

Experts from outside the organization will ideally bring both technical qualifications and objectivity to the review and possibly new perspectives that the author had not considered. External experts need only be active in the same subject area or be specialized in learning if insights in that domain are also desired. Engaging external experts may require additional funding and budgeting.

3.3.6 Crowd-sourced review

Crowd-sourcing is becoming increasingly popular for review and quality control. The idea is to rely on a larger group of users to suggest potential changes or make improvements to a knowledge asset. A familiar example of such a collaborative approach is the Wikipedia website, where one or several authors create a document, which is then gradually improved by a larger group of authors. Collaborative review may include a group of staff members within the organization or external users of the knowledge assets such as clients or external peers. Typical validation processes include reporting inappropriate content, rating usefulness, offering comments, and, in the case of wikis, editing the content.

3.4 Validation Methodologies

The four most common validation methods for knowledge assets are (1) testing them in a real-life setting, (2) organizing a review space, (3) checking against validation criteria, and (4) verifying with the initial experts or authors whether the knowledge asset is correctly described (figure 3.2). A fifth method, "six thinking hats," requires assessment of multiple perspectives on the validity of the asset.

Figure 3.2 Alternative Validation Methodologies

3.4.1 Putting the knowledge asset to the test

When it is feasible and does not put lives or property at risk, testing the asset—asking peers to apply its recommendations to address a similar challenge—can provide the most meaningful insights into the validity of a knowledge asset.

3.4.2 Organizing a review space for stakeholders and peers

Reviews by stakeholders and peers can occur as physical meetings, including in the form of focus groups; as individual interviews; or online through voting and feedback tools. Other forms of feedback can include online "liking," ranking, voting, and recommending.

3.4.3 Checking against predetermined criteria

Organizations can assess the value of a knowledge object against predetermined criteria. The *Knowledge Asset Validation Checklist* found in Useful Tools and Templates offers a starting point for this methodology.

3.4.4 Interviewing the authors

Interviews conducted in face-to-face conversations can help verify the expertise of the original experts or authors and how well the experiences were translated into conclusions and recommendations. The organization's content experts are best positioned to carry out these interviews.

3.4.5 Additional approach: Six thinking hats

This method allows a look at validity from six different angles. The methodology can be performed by six individuals or groups, each taking one perspective, or a single person can look at the knowledge asset from six different perspectives:

1. *Weaknesses.* Does the knowledge asset have particular weaknesses or can it be misunderstood? Is the knowledge asset complete in terms of its data?
2. *Content strengths.* What are the strengths of the knowledge asset and where will it be most useful?
3. *Accessible language.* Is the material clearly written?
4. *Linkages.* What other (existing/future) information does the knowledge asset relate to?
5. *Alternatives.* What would be alternative examples to illustrate or complement the knowledge asset?
6. *In totality.* Is the knowledge asset overall acceptable or does it require more work?

If the various perspectives are taken on by six individuals, they will present their findings to the rest of the group for discussion. Once all members are in agreement, the knowledge asset can be approved or sent back to the author for further revision.

3.5 Regular Review and Updates

To keep a high-quality repository of relevant knowledge, it is important to regularly review approved knowledge assets to ensure their continued validity. Remember, validation is a dynamic process that continues throughout the lifecycle of a knowledge asset. Because contexts may change and new insights can influence previously accepted conclusions and recommendations, the validity of knowledge assets can change as well. Some assets may already be outdated by the time they make it onto the knowledge-sharing platform; others can be highly relevant for years. To fortify a review regimen, it may even make sense to institute a "graveyard policy" that specifies a date by which each asset is presumed no longer valid and will either have to be removed or updated.

Set up continuous review cycles. In order to ensure that knowledge assets continue to be relevant it can be useful to institute a review schedule for each asset. You may choose to have each knowledge asset reviewed at least once a year, preferably by its author or a centralized review team. Also helpful for continuous quality control is crowd-sourced review, which allows users to comment on or rate the value of the knowledge asset. This in turn can trigger an update. If you choose to have knowledge assets created in a more dynamic environment such as a wiki, users may directly propose changes and updates.

3.6 Useful Tools and Templates

Table 3.1 Checklist for Validators

Question	Yes	No
Is the operational experience or lesson learned a valuable contribution to the operational practice?		
Does the knowledge asset address a distinct issue or challenge?		
Is the content correct?		
Is it presented clearly, so that it cannot be misinterpreted?		
Is the formal presentation and formatting of the content adequate?		

> continued

Table 3.1 Continued

Question	Yes	No
Is the language clear and appropriate?		
Is enough context provided for understanding the particular circumstances in which the operational experience occurred?		
Are concrete lessons and recommendations included?		
Does the knowledge asset create any risk, including reputational or regarding use of intellectual property?		
Other criteria?		

3.7 The Output

The validation process can yield approval or rejection of the proposed knowledge asset. A possible intermediate step before reaching either result is that the reviewers identify a number of needed revisions and either make the changes themselves or send the asset back to the authors for modification.

Once approved, the knowledge asset can be formatted for uploading to the knowledge platform or for use in knowledge and learning products.

3.8 Checklist for Designing the Validation Step

Question	Yes
Have we defined clear validation criteria?	
Have we decided on which validation arrangements to put in place?	
Have we defined the clearance procedures?	
In the case of validation by peers, external experts, or a validation committee, have we selected, invited, and briefed the reviewers?	
Have we defined the post-review processes for potential alterations?	

STEP 4: FORMATTING

4.1   Why Is Formatting Important?

At this stage the knowledge asset is almost complete. It has been reviewed, and its insights for operational solutions have been deemed valuable. The next step, formatting, is important because it allows others interested in the subject matter to easily find the material, especially when the organization's digital library contains dozens or even hundreds of other knowledge assets. Formatting also applies the organization's chosen standard for presenting the content of knowledge assets, which means readers can browse quickly to find information without having to first grasp a possibly unusual structure. Thus, formatting must be done before posting the knowledge asset in a repository.

Formatting at BNPB

The Indonesian Disaster Management Authority BNPB systematically captures lessons learned. It uploads the resulting knowledge assets to a central knowledge-sharing platform, the national Disaster Management Solutions Finder. Careful formatting and tagging of the respective knowledge assets before posting allows staff members and selected partners to access them online using either of two search functions—standard text search and expert search. The standard search looks for keywords, whereas the expert search looks for more specific tags, such as the author's department, project name, date when the experience

> continued

> continued from the previous page

was recorded, or stakeholder group involved. A complete set of metadata for each knowledge asset is particularly relevant, as the Disaster Management Solutions Finder also works as an expert locater. Some users may want further information from the author or other relevant stakeholders. In such cases, contact information becomes critical.

Formatting at Swachh Bharat Mission (SBM)

Given that most of its captured knowledge is currently documented via video, the SBM team uses metatagging as the main means of formatting. Under a carefully designed taxonomy, metatags include, for example, location (state, district, and block), type of category (e.g., children and youth; toilet technology; hygiene and handwashing; community engagement; solid and liquid waste management), names of capturing teams or team members, and date. Contained in a separate file, the metatags are given to the district magistrate in charge of validating and uploading the knowledge asset to the central knowledge repository.

4.2 The Process

Formatting involves two fundamental tasks: (1) organizing the content and the components of the asset and (2) adding qualifying information to make the knowledge asset findable. These task ensure that knowledge assets appear in a consistent and user-friendly manner and that its major content characteristics can be used to search for it. As discussed in chapter 2, the content should follow a logical sequence or cohesive storyline and highlight the key messages the author wants to convey. If the asset contains several disparate pieces of media, such as written material, video recordings, and images, they also should be assembled in a logical way to make them accessible.

4.2.1 Organizing the content

Operational experiences and lessons learned can be formatted in many different ways. The most frequently used formats for knowledge assets are documents (text, images, and graphics), presentations (slide shows with text, images, graphs, video, audio, and possibly some interaction), and video. The Global Development Research Center counts no less than 158 formats, including abstracts, videos, websites, white papers, workbooks, and working papers. Some formats focus on the media (example: video), and some on the content of the message (white paper). Some use graphics to

Table 4.1 Appropriate Uses for Knowledge Assets, by Asset Format

Format	Target Audience			Environment		Content		Media	
	Media	Experts	Students/ Junior Staff	Office	Field-based	Stable	Volatile	Multi-media	Text Only
Text-based document	x	x	x	x	x	x	x		x
Presentation		x	x	x		x	x	x	
Video	x	x	x	x		x		x	

deliver the message (map), others use text (report). Some present the content in lists or summaries (abstract), others use a narrative (story). Some formats are specifically developed for online distribution (website), others offline (book), and some are appropriate for both environments.

With so many options, choosing the appropriate format can be overwhelming. To guide your selection, keep in mind who will be using the knowledge asset and what their operating environment might be (table 4.1). It helps to consider how and in which context the knowledge asset will eventually be used and who will benefit from the lessons emerging from an operational experience.

The formatting possibilities for users in an office featuring good web connectivity will differ greatly from the options for field-based use, which may require more mobile-oriented and less data-heavy formats. Formatting for polished official communications differs from that acceptable for more technical or informal knowledge products.

Highly topical content that is likely to change quickly will require formats that can easily be adapted and edited, while basic or foundational knowledge can be formatted in more elaborate ways, possibly using audio-visual technologies or even interactive formats.

Use these guiding questions to help you choose:

» What are the characteristics of the target audience (type, size, preparedness)?
» In what environment are users likely to operate (access to technology, expectations on presentation quality)?
» How stable or volatile is the content (foundational knowledge or frequently changing)?
» In what types of formats does the captured material reside?
» What is the medium through which the content will likely be delivered?

If the knowledge asset was captured following the storyline proposed in chapter 2, formatting will now be quite straight-forward as you will have likely recorded the needed knowledge in the right sequence.

4.2.2 Making the knowledge asset searchable and findable

A quest for information on the Internet involves using a search engine whose results are links that may contain the material you want. Search engines use algorithms that use a combination of text search, metadata search, and other criteria such as frequency of use to select the results. The search engine on your organization's intranet will behave in a similar way, looking for keywords in the title or text of the knowledge asset or for qualifiers that you specify.

While uploading and sharing a few knowledge assets is not complicated, the task becomes more complex when uploading dozens or possibly hundreds of assets over time. The more assets you accumulate, the more difficult it will be to find specific information. Adding qualifiers, otherwise known as metadata or metatags, to the knowledge asset allows it to be found by a search engine. Metatags might specify the anticipated or most likely audience (e.g., disaster responders), the geographic location of the experience, and the date it occurred. But you may include many other qualifiers to enhance findability.

4.3 Useful Tools

Figure 4.1 presents a list of common qualifiers, or metatags.

4.4 The Output

When you have completed the formatting process, you are ready to upload the knowledge asset into a central knowledge library or repository. It can be published and made available to a wide audience interested in learning from the experience and possibly in replicating it in another context. The knowledge asset may also serve as a basis for other knowledge and learning products. For this, it will likely be combined with other related knowledge assets and possibly enhanced with additional information. The process of transforming a group of knowledge assets into knowledge and learning products is what we call *packaging* the knowledge.

Figure 4.1 Common Metatags for Searchability

- Title
- Short description
- Authors
- Date of publication
- Expiration date ("do not use after")
- Location (site, region, country, etc.)
- Georeference data
- Target area or coverage (the target area to which this knowledge applies)
- Type of media (document, video, presentation, etc.)
- Object format (Word file, PDF, WMV, PowerPoint, etc.)
- Size (number of pages, duration, number of slides, etc.)
- Size (e.g., megabytes)
- Domain-specific descriptors (use organizational taxonomy)
- Target audience (sector specialist, senior management, academia, public, etc.)
- Keywords
- Related materials
- Sources (references)
- Persons to contact for further information (and means of contact)
- Remarks
- Part of (if part of a series, give name of the series)
- Comes after (if another knowledge object logically precedes this object, indicate)
- Comes before (if another knowledge asset logically follows this asset, indicate)
- Status (draft/finished, public/restricted access)
- Validation by (name of person or team)

4.5 Checklist for Designing the Formatting Step

Question	Yes
Is a standardized formatting process in place that can be applied to all knowledge assets?	
Does the formatting process factor in the constraints of the audience that will use them and the environment in which they will be accessed?	
Does the knowledge asset contain all the information necessary for others to replicate the experience if they desired?	
Are the various components of the knowledge asset organized in a clear and accessible way?	
Have the common metatags been defined to increase searchability in the knowledge repository?	

STEP 5: PACKAGING FOR LEARNING AND SCALING UP

5.1 Why Is Packaging Knowledge Important?

Presentation is critical. Professionals are solutions-oriented, and time matters, so knowledge needs to be accessible, relevant, and quickly comprehensible to be useful. Poorly crafted knowledge assets can become unwanted noise, possibly even distracting us from discovering the right solution path. The literature on adult learning confirms this notion: adults seek learning not for general growth purposes but to complete specific operational tasks or fulfill social roles.[3] The immediate relevance of knowledge for application and replication is much more critical in adult work settings than in academic settings. An organization dedicated to capturing and sharing knowledge needs specialized staffing to succeed (see appendix E for examples of job descriptions).

Traditionally, important knowledge was disseminated through reports and case studies, but these long-form presentations are not always the best for on-the-job learning and decision making. Especially in situations that require that require fast action, professionals will not have time to read a 50-page case study to find the one bit of information they really need. Knowledge needs to be adequately *packaged* to make it usable for those who need it.

---

[3] See, for example, Knowles, Holton, and Swanson (2012).

In addition to the issue of packaging the information, the question of how the user will engage with the content is critical. How do we make sure the recipients of the knowledge understand it? How do they *learn*? Learning offerings are usually built around two components: (1) the content and (2) the activities that engage the audience with the content. For professionals to learn, both the learning materials and their delivery need to meet the above expectations. Packaging the content is the subject of this chapter. As for the activities, section 5.2.2 includes a list of "Top 10 Tips" that offer both packaging and presentation suggestions. The World Bank handbook *Becoming a Knowledge-Sharing Organization* (2016) provides further useful guidance on how to use packaged knowledge assets to create high-impact learning offerings.

Packaging Knowledge Assets for Learning at LAMATA

The Lagos Metropolitan Area Transport Authority (LAMATA) is a growing organization with an expanding mandate and scope of work. A continuous stream of new employees must be introduced to the organization, and current staff members may need to learn new skills. In addition, LAMATA risks the loss of important knowledge when core workers leave. Recognizing the value of staff members' knowledge, LAMATA started to capture and package knowledge assets derived from its own operational experiences and is using them to build learning offerings for classroom training, skills development, and e-learning. Besides their exposure to mentoring programs and international learning, LAMATA staff members are now increasingly being trained with these in-house learning products.

Packaging Knowledge for Learning and Scaling Up at Swachh Bharat Mission (SBM)

At SBM, captured experiences—typically via video—feed into a variety of knowledge-sharing activities and products. Video knowledge assets are shown at a variety of trainings and other gatherings to educate local residents and inspire them with the accomplishments of their peers in other communities. Audiences participate in discussions and debates over how to replicate or adapt the solutions presented. As SBM solutions multiply over time, they will support larger conferences, seminars, and cross-state peer learning events. Printed publications are planned to further showcase local experiences. Lastly, the SBM team expects that the captured knowledge will also form the basis for further analysis and research on strategies to overcome the sanitation challenge in India.

5.2 The Process: Packaging

Packaging knowledge assets into learning products is more of an art than a science. We know when knowledge captures our interest and gets us thinking. We also know when a presentation or publication does not grab our attention but rather makes our mind wander off. In this chapter we will cover packaging for the two most common uses of knowledge assets: in publications and in presentations. Whether designing them for publications or presentations, make knowledge assets engaging by packaging them with the following characteristics:

- Succinct and to the point
- Interesting, even intriguing
- Provoking reflection and reaction
- Application-oriented
- Well sequenced
- Built to reach a set of specific (learning) objectives
- Oriented toward a particular audience
- Professional looking
- Easy to understand, avoiding jargon
- Produced in a language that the user is comfortable with

5.2.1 Packaging for publication

Knowledge products can come in a wide variety of formats—the question is, which one is best for the need at hand? Imagine the following scenario: You are staying at a hotel on an upper floor. Suddenly the fire alarm goes off. You have to quickly decide what to do, and you have the following knowledge products to help you choose the best course of action (figure 5.1): (1) a case study on hotel fires and evacuation procedures, (2) an emergency evacuation plan for the hotel, and (3) a list of phone numbers of friends, one of whom is a fire fighter. Which is best suited to helping you quickly get out of the hotel?

In situations that require fast action, professionals will not have time to read a 50-page case study to find the one bit of information they really need. Knowledge needs to be adequately *packaged* to make it usable for those who need it.

Figure 5.1 Which Publication Will Best Help You Get Out of a Burning Hotel?

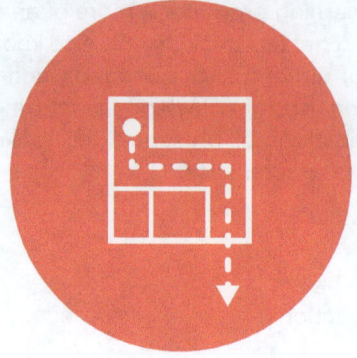

Case study on hotel fires and evacuation procedures

Emergency evacuation plan for the hotel

Phone list including friend who is a fire fighter

Surely it is item 2. The emergency evacuation plan that is posted at the entrance to your room will give you the information you need to most efficiently get to safety. That does not mean that the other options are always bad; they are just not the most appropriate for that specific circumstance. A case study can be a valuable source of learning for fire fighters and hotel staff to better understand hotel safety procedures. A phone directory that provides access to a variety of specialists can be an incredibly useful tool for multiple circumstances.

What may seem trivial is often easily overlooked when we are tasked with developing a knowledge product as a publication. We need to first fully understand the circumstances in which it will be used, what purpose it is intended to serve, and whom it is for.

The 5W-1H questions (figure 5.2) can lead us to the critical answers needed to develop targeted, high-impact publications:

- » Who is the publication for?
- » What information and knowledge is most relevant for the audience?
- » Where will it be used?
- » When will it be used?
- » Why is it important to have?
- » How will it be used?

Knowledge assets can be used in a wide variety of publications. The following are among the most common:

Figure 5.2 The 5W-1H Questionnaire

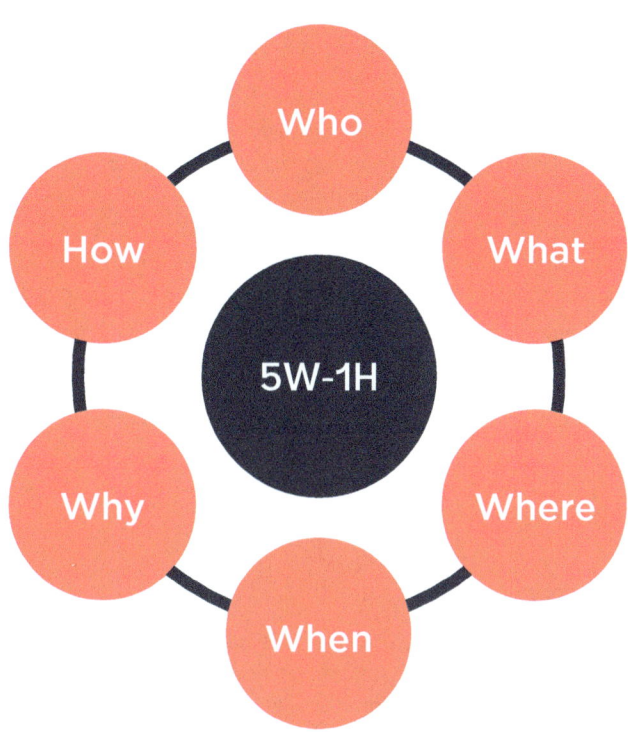

Guidance notes

Short guidance notes can be a practical way to convey how-to knowledge to staff members and partners. As always, be succinct and enrich the note, when possible, with illustrations or graphs that help boil down the information even further. Step-by-step lists (in the case of linear processes) and checklists can be helpful. Depending on their use, the guidance notes can be part of a collection that is regularly expanded, and they can also be made available online. A folded-leaflet format can also be appropriate so users can easily carry it with them. Because only the most critical information is in the notes, they should contain pointers on where to get additional information.

Encouraging Organizational Learning: IFC SmartLessons

The International Finance Corporation (IFC) founded the SmartLessons program in 2007 to capture its staff members' crucial how-to knowledge. Through the prism of their own experiences, both positive and negative, SmartLessons authors aim to capture practical lessons that can be useful for their colleagues working on similar projects or facing similar issues. A design toolkit guides practitioners through the process of capturing. It helps them avoid the technicalities of a project's subject matter and focus instead on decision processes and specific recommendations that are important and replicable. The SmartLessons team applies a rigorous approval process to all submissions, which can be in a written or video format, to ensure that the lessons will consistently add value to the knowledge of internal and external audiences. A series of SmartLessons that focus on a single topic area or region are sometimes compiled into SmartBooks (https://wdronline.worldbank.org/handle/10986/9412).

Case studies in learning offerings

In the context of learning offerings, knowledge assets can be used as case studies to supplement classroom or e-learning experiences, for example to convey a practical application of a guideline or concept. A two-page length is ideal for a given item—it enforces brevity and allows printing on a single sheet. And if you design the document with color, also consider how it will look if users reproduce it in black and white.

Learning from Experience with the Global Delivery Initiative

The Global Delivery Initiative (GDI) is an international effort to create a knowledge base of development know-how focused on implementation (http://www.globaldeliveryinitiative.org). Launched in 2015 and hosted at the World Bank, the project includes more than 40 partners, including government agencies, multilateral development banks, bilateral donors, universities, and nonprofit organizations.

GDI's work is centered on the premise that development interventions often encounter difficulties during implementation—capacity shortfalls, misaligned incentives, or lack of coordination among stakeholders, to name but a few. Technical solutions alone are not enough to navigate these complexities. Achieving transformational impact in a more consistent and timely manner requires better integration of the right technical "what" with the right delivery "how."

> continued from the previous page

GDI products include the Global Delivery Library, which allows practitioners to learn, adapt, and course-correct implementation as they learn how others have addressed the same challenges they face. The library's resources include case studies, delivery notes, a video-hypermedia platform with how-to information, and a toolkit for adaptive implementation. To support this knowledge-capturing approach, the GDI has developed a methodology for producing case studies, and writers around the world have been trained to use it.

Communications for organizational outreach

Many organizations package knowledge assets to conduct outreach. The assets are typically chosen for the notable results they describe, but adding solution paths could provide valuable insights, and including testimonials from stakeholders will aid credibility. Photographs can add impact, but avoid generic images in favor of pictures showing actual stakeholders and situations that illustrate a particular experience or results.

Research reports

A knowledge asset documents empirical information derived from actual experiences. As such, it might fit into formal, larger-scale research documents, for example as a part of new findings derived from emerging patterns. Research documents necessarily tend to be either long or highly compressed for a specialized audience. To more widely distribute the knowledge embedded in such reports, use the strategies applied in the steps for capturing and packaging knowledge assets: formulate a short synopsis of the key findings for quick consumption.

Policies and regulations

Consistent evidence from multiple knowledge assets can help policy makers fashion initiatives to scale up proven solution paths. Packaged to fit the needs of the policy documents, the knowledge assets can serve, for example, as background experience that supports the initiatives.

5.2.2 Packaging for presentations

Presentations to an audience are one of the most challenging knowledge-sharing tasks. As subject-matter experts, we often fall victim to the belief that all information is critical and that the devil is in the details—so we overload the presentation with far more text and graphs than an audience can possibly absorb. Such presentations are also more of a crutch for the presenter than a packaging of key messages that truly speak to the audience.

It takes practice to be selective, succinct, relevant, and focused while still being engaging. A few guiding principles can help you accomplish this difficult task:

- Identify and feature the "must know" information.
- Keep the "nice to know" information in the background so it doesn't overshadow the essential content.
- Be problem- and solution-oriented.
- Keep the audience and the learning objectives in mind at all times.
- Present material in different ways, for example by adding audiovisual components. Sometimes just a picture can do wonders to enrich a message.

Top 10 Tips for packaging and presentations

The following tips offer some more-specific key strategies for both packaging knowledge and designing high-impact presentations:

1. **Determine the audience and purpose**

   A presentation should always have a clear purpose. Before working on the slides, think through what you want to achieve, who the audience is, and what their expectations are. The 5W-1H questionnaire will help you determine some of the key information you need before starting: "Who, what, where, when, why, and how?"

2. **Structure your presentation around key messages**

   A good presentation follows a sound storyline—a simple script that the audience will understand. Here's a way to create it: Decide on the order in which the key messages will appear. Give each key message a headline and put each headline on its own slide with no other text or images just yet. Read each headline aloud and in order. Does the narrative flow well? This is an efficient way to discover any need for adjustments in sequence or message content.

3. **Create interest**

   Consider starting with some attention-grabbing element—a question, fun fact, image, or short video—to quickly involve your audience in the presentation.

4. **Develop the graphic layout**

   Use a professional-looking graphic template for your slides—generic versions supplied by the presentation software are usually inadequate. Help promote your organization's brand by using its presentations template, usually featuring its logo, corporate colors, and the typeface used in its other communication products. If your organization does not have a template, consider engaging a graphic designer to create one that leaves enough space for the slide content, does not compete for attention, and includes page numbers. For the content itself, be sure font size both for headlines and text is large enough to be readable from the back of the presentation room.

5. **Keep it simple**

    The golden rule for presentations is one key message per slide. This sounds easier than it is; we are usually tempted to put as much information on a page as possible. Your ability to resist this temptation will have a big impact on the success of your presentation.

6. **Use the presentation for support, not for the full narrative**

    Your talking points will be more extensive than what appears on the slides. Put the talking points in the notes section of each slide to use as a reference during your presentation. If instead your slides contain long bulleted lists or whole sentences and paragraphs, your audience will stop listening to you and just read what is on the screen—if indeed the text isn't too small to be readable! In any case, your audience came to listen to you, not read (see figures 5.4 and 5.5).

7. **Select your images carefully**

    You know the saying: A picture is worth a thousand words. That is certainly true for presentations. Images can be a powerful complement to your narrative. They enforce key messages and help your audience remember them. Don't use the stock images supplied by your presentation application. They usually don't look professional and have been over-used by others already. When possible, use your own photos, illustrations, and graphs. Image search engines and professional stock-image libraries also provide a vast range of excellent material (be careful to respect the copyrights).

8. **Simplify graphs and tables**

    If you have to present numbers, find ways to make the message obvious. Large tables with lots of numbers do not work. For example, consider highlighting key comparisons in a table or using arrows or highlighting to identify key areas of a graph. As with everything in your presentation, the "less is more" rule applies. Bar charts can be visually more compelling when comparing numbers. As with the text, font sizes for graphs and tables will need to be large enough to be readable throughout the presentation room.

9. **Avoid animated transitions and effects**

    It is tempting to use the many fancy animations, dissolves, spins, and transitions provided in most presentation applications. They may look impressive or entertaining at first, but they quickly get annoying and distract from the actual narrative and key messages. It is best to avoid animations and sound effects altogether.

10. **Keep it fun, light, and engaging**

    Good presentations engage the audience from start to finish. They allow for reflection, moments of surprise, and interactivity. Build in questions and short anecdotes. Keeping your audience's interest is not simple, but by applying the key rules discussed here, you dramatically increase your chance of giving a successful presentation.

5.2.3 Designing a text slide

An example of what to avoid in creating a text slide (figure 5.3) is a long list of characteristics for knowledge assets. On a slide, such detailed content is unreadable—thus, virtually useless—and would be better communicated in a handout.

Figure 5.3 The Unreadable List

Descriptors for Knowledge Assets

Title:
- Short description:
- Author(s):
- Date of publication (DD MM YYYY):
- Expiry date: do not use after (DD MM YYYY):
- Location (site, region, country…):
- Target area or coverage:
- Type of object(s) (document, video, presentation, etc):
- Object format (Word doc, pdf, wmv, ppt, etc):
- Language(s):
- Size (number of pages, duration, number of slides):
- Domain specific descriptor 1 [work area, use organizational taxonomy]
- Domain specific descriptor 2
- Target audience [sector specialist, senior management, academia, public, etc.):
- Keywords:
- Related materials [references to other materials/knowledge objects that may be of interest]:
- Sources (references):
- Resource person(s):
- Comes before and after [sequence of knowledge objects in a series – where applicable]:
- Remarks:
- Part of a series (where applicable):
- Status [draft/finished, open/restricted access]:
- Validation date and validated by:

A better visual approach to the same content would be selectivity—giving only the most important information (figure 5.4). The reduction in the number of words allows for larger type and for visible color variations that further improve readability. More available space also allows for a more informative title.

Figure 5.4 Selectivity for Readability

> **Provide additional information to make knowledge assets findable.**
>
> Author   Location
> Topic
> Date   Language

Be selective. We can only take in a limited amount of information in a given time, so don't overwhelm your audience with too much data, or they'll suffer an information overdose.

Carefully select and pace your content to ensure learning. (Easier said than done!) Given the vast amount of knowledge available, it's easy to create an overly long and dense presentation. It is much harder to present what really matters and drive home a few key concepts—all of which is the information you want the audience to remember from the learning offering.

Distinguish between "must know" and "nice to have" as you prepare your materials. Cut out the information that is not necessary to have, then build activities around the "must" information. When in doubt, you can layer the content so that "must know" knowledge is required or featured, whereas the nice-to-have may be referenced, linked, or put in an annex.

5.3 The Output

We have arrived at the end of the five-step process leading us from identifying to packaging knowledge assets. You now have the tools and know-how to develop publications and presentations that successfully use captured experiences for learning.

Remember, however, that the process outlined in this guide is only suggestive. Variation in practice is almost inevitable, and the order of steps presented here will not always work. Also, capturing is an iterative process, so you may often find yourself going back and forth between the various steps. Continuous validation and testing with your audience will help you keep your learning products relevant.

5.4 Checklist for Designing the Packaging Step

Question	Yes
Are we clear about the audience for whom we want to package the knowledge?	
Are we clear about why, when, and how the audience be would likely to use the knowledge product?	
Have we defined whether the knowledge product will be used for publication or presentation purposes?	
Is the format of the knowledge product the most appropriate for its intended use?	
Have we factored in the constraints the audience will face in trying to access the packaged knowledge product?	
Have we defined quality criteria for knowledge products and does the knowledge product meet them?	

APPENDIXES

A. Identification Templates

1. Knowledge evaluation questionnaire
2. 5W-1H knowledge identification questionnaire
3. Sample knowledge audit survey
4. Organizational knowledge gap analysis
5. Individual skills gap analysis

B. Knowledge-Capturing Activities

1. Interview
2. Storytelling
3. Observation
4. Blog
5. After-action review
6. Focus group
7. Wiki
8. Collaborative workspace
9. Webinar
10. Online forum
11. Community of practice

C. Capturing with Video
1. The sound
2. The image

D. Examples of Knowledge Assets
1. Indonesia's National Disaster Management Authority (BNPB)
2. Nigeria's Lagos Metropolitan Area Transport Authority (LAMATA)
3. Swachh Bharat ("Clean India") Mission (SBM)

E. Functions and Terms of Reference
1. Knowledge-Sharing Steering Committee
2. Knowledge-Management/Knowledge-Sharing Coordination Team
3. Chief Knowledge and Learning Officer
4. Knowledge and Learning Specialist
5. Knowledge-Capturing Specialist
6. Audiovisual Media Specialist

A. Identification Templates

1. Knowledge evaluation questionnaire
2. 5W-1H knowledge identification questionnaire
3. Sample knowledge audit survey
4. Organizational knowledge gap analysis
5. Individual skills gap analysis

A.1 Knowledge evaluation questionnaire

This questionnaire can help determine whether the knowledge object (the practical experience, lesson learned, or practice) is worth capturing, keeping, and sharing.

The questionnaire would preferably be answered by the person who identifies the experience or practice, but it can also be answered by others (experts, colleagues, researchers, trainers, knowledge workers, managers, etc.) tasked with assessing the value of the knowledge for replication. If the answer is "No" to all or most of questions, then there is no apparent justification for capturing this experience. If the knowledge gained from the experience passes this test, you can move to the next step: the actual knowledge capture itself, beginning typically with application of the 5W-1H knowledge identification questionnaire (section A.2).

Knowledge Evaluation Questionnaire

	Yes	No
Do you know someone who can or will use the lesson learned from this experience or event?		
Has there already been an explicit demand for this specific knowledge, practice or lesson learned?		
Are professionals in identical or in similar situations asking or looking for this knowledge?		
Is it clear to you what challenge the experience addresses?		
Do you know if this experience fills a known knowledge gap?		
Can the experience and the lessons learned be recorded?		
Is the expert able and willing to express his lesson learned verbally, in text, images, sound, video or other media?		
Can the experience and the lessons learned be shared?		

> continued

> continued from the previous page

	Yes	No
Is this lesson or practice replicable and reusable?		
Is the knowledge generic enough to be of interest to others besides the expert?		
Can others effectively understand it and learn from it?		
Is there a chance that the knowledge gained in the experience will ever be needed again?		
Is it likely that the same or a similar professional situation will occur again, to the expert or to others?		
Can the information that you need to collect be shared with your target audience?		

A.2   5W-1H knowledge identification questionnaire

The 5W-1H (who, what, when, where, why, how) questionnaire helps gather information about the experience or lesson learned. The information does not yet need to be comprehensive, but it should include enough data to evaluate the usefulness of the experience for others.

Usually the person who considers an experience or event useful for capturing will be the one filling out the questionnaire. This can be the expert, a colleague or an external person (for example a knowledge worker, trainer or researcher) involved with capturing and managing knowledge in the organization. Involving people who participated in the experience or event is useful. We recommend completing the questionnaire within 24 hours of the event or experience, or as soon as possible after, to avoid losing important background information. Hence the answers to this questionnaire might be quickly sketched in before the evaluative questionnaire (section A.1) is answered.

Get a quick overview of an experience. Interview people who were directly involved in the experience or event. This step should take between 5 and 10 minutes. Provide enough detail to make the information useful for the rest of the process, but do not try to be exhaustive at this stage. You can adapt the form to your own situation or requirements. Use the 5W-1H questions to guide you.

5W-1H Knowledge Identification Questionnaire

Title	(Give a unique title to the experience/challenge)
Who	Who is it about?
	Who is involved?
	Who knows more about this?
	Who should learn about this?
	. . .?
What	What happened?
	What happened beforehand?
	What happened afterwards?
	What did you do?
	What did you not do?
	What did others do?
	What did others not do?
	What did you learn from this?
	What is the impact of this event or experience?
	. . .?
When	When did it take place?
	When did it begin?
	When did it stop?
	When did you get involved?
	When do you need this information?
	. . .?
Where	Where did it take place?
	Where did you come from?
	Where did you go to?
	Where were the others?
	Where do you want to find this information?
	. . .?

> continued

> continued from the previous page

Title	(Give a unique title to the experience/challenge)
Why	Why did it happen? Why did it begin? Why did it stop? Why did you do what you did? Why do you need to share this experience? ...?
How	How did you feel about what happened? How did other people feel about it? ...?

A.3 Sample knowledge audit survey

Sample Knowledge Audit Survey

Rate the responses from 5 (most typical) to 1 (least typical)

When a colleague asks you to help with their knowledge needs, what type of knowledge is typically sought?	Essential for performance, improving the service, the operations	5 - 4 - 3 - 2 - 1
	Essential for the organization's strength	5 - 4 - 3 - 2 - 1
	Important for safer, better, innovative or creative ways of working	5 - 4 - 3 - 2 - 1
	Outdated and no longer useful	5 - 4 - 3 - 2 - 1
How did you acquire most of the skills and expertise that you have been using in your job over the past 6 months?	At work in this organization	5 - 4 - 3 - 2 - 1
	Through self-learning	5 - 4 - 3 - 2 - 1
	Through formal training	5 - 4 - 3 - 2 - 1
	At my last job or elsewhere	5 - 4 - 3 - 2 - 1
	From my colleagues	5 - 4 - 3 - 2 - 1

Where is most of the knowledge that you need to do your work located or stored?	In paper-based documents	5 – 4 – 3 – 2 – 1
	In our team/dept. members' heads	5 – 4 – 3 – 2 – 1
	In our central information system	5 – 4 – 3 – 2 – 1
	On my computer/hard drive	5 – 4 – 3 – 2 – 1
Who owns the knowledge that you acquire in your present job/organization?	Me alone	5 – 4 – 3 – 2 – 1
	The organization alone	5 – 4 – 3 – 2 – 1
	Depends on how much I had put in to it	5 – 4 – 3 – 2 – 1
	Both myself and the organization	5 – 4 – 3 – 2 – 1
How often do you make use of documented procedures to do your work when you are stuck?	Constantly—very often—quite often—not often/rarely—never	
Which of the following is the biggest barrier to the efficient and effective storage of the information you receive?	Lack of time/too busy	5 – 4 – 3 – 2 – 1
	Poor tools/technology	5 – 4 – 3 – 2 – 1
	Organization policy/directives	5 – 4 – 3 – 2 – 1
	Poor information systems/processes	5 – 4 – 3 – 2 – 1
How often do you formally share information with other similar organizations?	Constantly—very often—quite often—not often/rarely—never	
What are the challenges in sharing information with people from other organizations?	They/we (or both) don't perceive an urgent need to share	5 – 4 – 3 – 2 – 1
	Lack of open-minded sharing environment	5 – 4 – 3 – 2 – 1
	Lack of trust of other people's knowledge	5 – 4 – 3 – 2 – 1
	No proper organizational guidelines on sharing	5 – 4 – 3 – 2 – 1
	Bureaucratic procedure involved in sharing info/knowledge	5 – 4 – 3 – 2 – 1
	Task doesn't require cross-organizational information sharing	5 – 4 – 3 – 2 – 1
	No proper IT platform to share	5 – 4 – 3 – 2 – 1
	Do not know about other people's knowledge needs	5 – 4 – 3 – 2 – 1

A.4. Organizational knowledge gap analysis

Identify current and future knowledge needs in your organization. The information can be used to plan training and learning programs. Identifying current and expected future operational elements (the first table below) may be a helpful prelude to analyzing knowledge gaps.

Analysis of Operations at the Organizational Level

Operational Elements	Current		Future Required
	Existing	Required	
Functions	Existing functions in your organization	Functions needed to best deliver on current key outcomes	Functions needed to best deliver on future key outcomes
Key outcomes	Critical outcomes your organization currently needs to produce		Future outcomes that your organization should produce
Core competencies	Competencies that currently allow your organization to deliver on the above key outcomes	Competencies needed but lacking to deliver on the above key outcomes in your organization. This answer will inform measures to develop capacity and skills	Competencies needed to deliver on above future outcomes but lacking in your organization

Analysis of Knowledge Gaps at the Organizational and Individual Level

Knowledge Resources and Uses	Current		Future Required
	Existing	Required	
Major internal and external *types* of information and knowledge	All that you or your organization use (can include data files, reports, studies, video files, e-discussion threads, etc.)	All that you or your organization lack but need to ensure smooth operations (can include data files, reports, studies, video files, e-discussion threads, etc.)	All that you or your organization need to help deliver on future operational tasks
Major internal and external *sources* of information and knowledge	All that are currently being used by you or your organization	All that you or your organization lack but need to ensure smooth operations	All that you or your organization lack but need to meet future operational needs

Knowledge Resources and Uses	Current		Future Required
	Existing	Required	
Frequency of use of major internal and external *sources* of information and knowledge	*How often you or your organization currently uses the above sources*	*How often you or your organization should use (but don't) the above sources to ensure smooth operations*	*How often you or your organization will need to use the above sources to ensure smooth future operations*
Use of sources by key internal and external stakeholders	*All key stakeholders who are currently using the above sources*	*All key stakeholders who should use (but don't) the above sources to ensure smooth operations*	*All key stakeholders who will need to use the above sources to ensure smooth future operations*
Key processes: mechanisms, events, functionalities, or platforms to capture, manage, share, and find information	*Your organization: All that it currently uses* *You: All that you currently use*	*Your organization: All that it needs but lacks to meet current operational needs* *You: All that you need but lack to meet current operational needs*	*Your organization: All that it will need but currently lacks to meet future operational needs* *You: All that you will need but currently lack to meet future operational needs*
Major outcomes	*Your organization: All that it currently achieves by using the above sources and processes* *You: All that you achieve by using the above sources and processes*	*Your organization: All that it could achieve if it had the above missing sources and processes* *You: All that you could achieve if you had the above missing sources and processes*	*Your organization: All that it must achieve by using the above additional sources and processes* *You: All that you must achieve by using the above additional sources and processes*
Time spent per week, month or year on *formal* knowledge-sharing and learning activities	*Estimate of time you or your organizational unit currently spend*	*Estimate of time you or your organizational unit should spend to meet current operational needs*	*Estimate of time you or your organizational unit should spend to meet future operational needs*
Time spent on *informal* knowledge-sharing and learning activities (including water cooler talks, lunch conversations, phone calls, etc.)	*Estimate of time you or your organizational unit currently spend*	*Estimate of time you or your organizational unit should spend to meet current operational needs*	*Estimate of time you or your organizational unit should spend to meet future operational needs*
Time spent searching for critical knowledge	*Estimate of time you or your organizational unit currently spend*	*Estimate of time you or your organizational unit should spend to meet current operational needs if it had the above sources and processes*	*Estimate of time you or your organizational unit should spend to meet future operational needs if it had the above sources and processes*

A.5. Individual skills gap analysis

Use this template to assess your own or your staff members' competency levels. This information can be used to plan training and learning programs.

Key to the skills analysis tables:

Lack = full learning need.
Needs to improve = partial learning need.
Competent = no learning need.

Skills Analysis 1: Technical Skills on a Given Subject

Activity	Skill Level		
	Lack	Needs to Improve	Competent
[Example:] *Guide the development of public policies on [a given subject]*			
Etc.			

Skills Analysis 2: Cross-Cutting Functional Skills

Activity	Skill Level		
	Lack	Needs to Improve	Competent
[Examples:] *Project management* *Report writing* *Computer skills* *Presentations* *Quantitative analysis* *Engaging with francophone stakeholders in written and spoken French*			
Etc.			

Skills Analysis 3: Behavioral or Leadership Skills

Activity	Desired Behavior	Skill Level		
		Lack	Needs to Improve	Competent
[Examples:] Teamwork Client relations management Mentoring or coaching Participative process management Etc.	[Example: Teamwork] Putting the success of the team above one's own recognition			
Etc.				

B. Knowledge-Capturing Activities

1. Interview
2. Storytelling
3. Observation
4. Blog
5. After-action review
6. Focus group
7. Wiki
8. Collaborative workspace
9. Webinar
10. Online forum
11. Community of practice

B.1 Interview

The most direct way to find out what someone knows is to ask him or her. The interview is the most frequently used method for eliciting knowledge. The interviewer asks questions to discover facts and opinions related to an experience. Structured one-on-one interviews help provide information about observations, background knowledge, attitudes, and beliefs surrounding a particular experience. For best results, interviewers should prepare thoroughly, ideally creating a list of questions carefully arranged in a particular order, especially if more than one person will be interviewed sequentially about the same event. A set list of questions ensures that every participant is asked the same questions in more or less the same way, reducing bias.

Interviews can be captured on paper, with a voice recorder, or with a video camera. Interviews are usually done in person, although interviews by telephone or videoconferencing are also possible.

Tips and tricks for interviewing

Interviews have four stages: arrangement, preparation, interview, and reconstruction.

1. *Arrangement*

    A smooth interview process requires some advance logistical arrangements and communications.

    » Make an appointment with the interviewee(s) and describe the objective.
    » If several persons have to be interviewed, interview the principal person last.
    » Schedule the interview(s) and reserve a location that is quiet and has few distractions.
    » Send an invitation with the details of the interview (location, timing, topic, duration, etc.).
    » Call your respondents the day before the interview to remind them.

2. *Preparation*

    How one conducts the interview and asks questions has a huge impact on the quality of information obtained.

    » Begin preparation well in advance of the interview day.
    » Define what you want to get out of the interview.
    » Define your target interviewee and think why he or she was selected.
    » Define what type of interview it will be (survey, in-depth, guided, or conversation).
    » Research the event, fact, or experience as much as possible.
    » Prepare an appropriate introduction.
    » Create a topic list indicating the topics and specific questions you want to address during the interview. These topics can be related to behavior, opinions or values, feelings, knowledge, senses (what was seen, heard, observed, etc.), or standard background or demographic questions.

- » To preserve spontaneity, don't share questions with the interviewee in advance of the interview.
- » Make sure all issues are addressed.
- » Use the 5W-1H (what, why, who, when, where, and how) questions as guidance for the main part of the interview.
- » Test your interview questions to see if you are meeting your objectives.
- » Conclude the interview design with final questions or comments, follow up, etc.
- » Choose the right capturing technology (written, spoken, audio, or video recording).
- » If using recording equipment, set it up and test it in advance.

3. *The interview*

   Central to a good interview is first making your conversation partner feel comfortable and then getting him or her as involved in the conversation as possible.

   - » Welcome the respondent, introduce yourself, and start with casual conversation to create the right atmosphere. Make the respondent feel comfortable.
   - » Describe the steps of the interview process:
     - » Informed consent
     - » Interview session
     - » Answering their questions
     - » Incentive or reimbursement for the session
     - » Explanation of how you will use the results of the interview.
   - » Ideally, obtain informed consent orally now with recording equipment running, or in writing.
   - » Communicate the expected length and level of detail of the answers. If using recording equipment, ask the interviewee to convey the key message of his or her answer in the first minute, followed by further elaboration where needed.
   - » Begin to address all of the questions or topics and feel free to ask follow-up questions or questions triggered by the response to gain more insights in the topic, case, or experience.
   - » Ask short and relevant questions. Give the interviewee time to think and respond. Let interviewees explain what happened in their own words.
   - » Be a good listener.
   - » Keep eye contact and observe body language. Observe and document the behavior of your respondent and contextual aspects of the interview and take notes even if you are

using audiovisual equipment. You need only note keywords or points and elaborate on them after the interview is complete.

- Mix "heavy" questions with "light" questions, and fact-based with scenario-based questions.
- Try to remain neutral.
- Think of follow-up questions.
- Use the interview structure you prepared (5W-1H) and ask for specifics: how long, how many, what for, with whom, etc.
- Inquire about the interviewee's personal lessons learned.
- Give the interviewee the opportunity to ask questions.
- Thank your respondent.
- Note down any additional materials you need to collect, given the respondent's answers (images, photos, statistics, data, information from other experts, etc.).
- Expand your notes as soon as possible after each interview (preferably within 24 hours).

4. *Reconstruction*

After the interview, put the information into a form—perhaps a document or presentation illustrating the insights from the interview—that you can share and use later in the formatting process.

- Immediately after the interview, review your notes taken during the interview, and recap your thoughts and considerations even if you also used recording equipment. Otherwise, your memory will fade, even after one day, and some important notes may become meaningless.
- Make transcripts of the interview.
- Make a report of the interview. If you are carrying out several interviews (which is recommended) you can use the report of this first interview as a means to compare and contrast your results.
- Summarize the findings in key points and use quotes to illustrate and support your findings.

Advantages

The biggest advantage of interviewing is the depth of detail you can gain. Interviewees can paint lively pictures of what happened and give the interviewer a first-hand view of the event. The interviewer can tailor the questions to the respondent to elicit more examples or explanations. Interviews can be useful to capture background, root causes, and influencing factors in addition to describing what happened in a particular event. Interviews can also provide insight into the respondent's interpretations, perceptions, thoughts, and feelings, which may be conveyed through social cues such as intonation and body language.

Disadvantages

Recruiting people and making appointments for interviews can be challenging. You have to find a convenient place and time and may have to coordinate multiple calendars. Interviewers may forget to ask key questions, or answers may later spark new questions; but once the interview is over, it may be hard to later follow-up with the subject. At times too much information is collected, which makes later processing very time-consuming.

A special case: Exit interviews

When individuals leave the organization, managers conduct exit interviews to help assess what should be improved or changed, reduce the loss of knowledge that the departure might entail, and to help new staff members so that they will not have to "reinvent the wheel."

Typical exit interview questions:

- What is the most important lesson you learned from professional experiences with clients? With colleagues? With management?
- What was your biggest success/failure in the organization and why?
- What single most important recommendation would you give to management? To colleagues? To your successor?
- Could you give an anecdote that provides an important insight for our current or new staff?
- If you could make one change, what would it be?
- Which immediate priority actions that your successor should work on and what would be your advice on those actions?
- Which current organizational assets or arrangements are important to preserve?
- Which tools, knowledge resources, and relationships were most important for you in performing your job? What was missing?

B.2 Storytelling

Storytelling is a useful way to share information and generate understanding. It is increasingly being used by organizations to share and interpret experiences in a social context. From the perspective of a listener, it is easier to understand and remember knowledge when it is presented as a story. Moreover, storytelling can supplement analytical thinking—an expert may not realize the full value of an experience until he or she tells the story.

How to tell the story

If you are telling the story, bear in mind these recommendations to generate valuable knowledge:

- Define the key message of the story.
- Build the right atmosphere for storytelling.

- » Build the story on your own experience: use keywords if necessary to guide the story and to keep on track.
- » Start by providing the necessary context, and conclude with lessons learned and recommendations, if any.
- » Observe the listeners while telling the story.

How to listen to the story

- » Show your interest and curiosity.
- » Listen carefully—be receptive, comprehending, and responsive.
- » Let the story carry you away—don't interrupt, and hold questions until the end.

B.3 Observation

Much knowledge can be obtained simply by observing experts performing their work. Observation provides an overview of their expertise or particular experience. It can generate a basic understanding of the knowledge involved as well as of constraints or other issues.

Observations ideally occur in the expert's working environment, so observers see actual behavior. However, not all relevant experiences (such as accidents or unexpected events) can be observed. Observation methodology varies depending on the subject of the observation, the role of the observer (participatory or passive), and the recording method (writing, photos, audio or video).

Advantages

Nonintrusive or nonparticipatory observation interferes minimally with the expert's practice and can provide insight on facts, rules, and strategies that experts adopt, even those the experts are unaware of.

Disadvantages

It is often difficult to remain unbiased and objective when analyzing observations. Also, the interpretation can be time-consuming because of the amount of data collected.

B.4 Blog

A blog is a website created by an individual or group and is accessible either to the public or to members of a closed community. The blog consists of text contributions ("blog posts") by the person or group that created the site; it works like a diary, allowing the blogger to write down experiences informally, and also as a direct (unedited) channel of communication with an audience.

Advantages

- » Setting up and using a blog is quite easy, even for those who are not very digitally literate.
- » Blogs usually don't cost anything.

- Publishing a blog post is usually instantaneous because blogs do not have a publisher or content gatekeeper (although the blog creator may monitor comments by readers for appropriateness or bar comments altogether).
- They accommodate text, images, video, and links to web pages or other blogs.
- They are easy to update.
- They are easy to access, provided an Internet connection is available.
- They encourage storytelling as a way of transferring knowledge.
- Readers can leave feedback and thus interact with the blogger.

Disadvantages

- Blogs can be biased or contain inaccuracies.
- Writing a blog can be time-consuming.
- Visitors may leave inappropriate comments.
- Bloggers often don't widely promote the existence of their blog, in which cases a blog's readership is not as large or diverse as it could be.

B.5 After-action review

An after-action review (AAR) is conducted by a moderator with a team as soon as possible after it has experienced an operation or event. The goal is to give the team members an opportunity to reflect on the action so that they can do better the next time.

How to conduct an after-action review

AARs are ideally taken immediately after the event. At that moment, memory is still fresh and authentic (that is, unfiltered by later interpretations or judgments) and those who participated in the experience are still available. AARs are typically held face-to-face, but can be held virtually as well.

A moderator leads the review, posing questions such as these:

- What was planned? What was supposed to happen?
- Was the actual occurrence different from what was planned? Wanted here are facts, not judgments.
- Why were there differences?
- What went well and why?
- What can be improved and how? What can we do differently in the future?

The unique value of an AAR is the opportunity it provides to obtain reliable qualitative knowledge when it is most fresh. The key to the success of an AAR is to have an open discussion in which all understand that the goal is to learn and fix problems, not to blame. Therefore, AARs are held without any spectators. Participants must feel free to interact and express themselves without regard to formal hierarchies.

People often record AAR discussions on flip charts during the review, then later process the notes into learning objects and insights for others in the organization or elsewhere.

B.6 Focus group

Focus groups can be effective for recording and evaluating experiences and perceptions. A focus group is made up of experts and other stakeholders who were or will be involved in a particular experience; their group discussion can yield a great deal of information and insight. The group setting allows participants to respond and build on others' suggestions or comments. Focus groups about a past event should be held as soon as possible to obtain feedback that will help practitioners develop new procedures and plans for the future. Focus groups are typically conducted in-person, but holding them through telephone or video conferencing may sometimes be necessary.

Preparation

Your level of preparation will largely determine the value of the focus group's results. If you do some advance planning for focus groups to be held with designated teams even for quick follow-up after unexpected events, you will be able to use most if not all of the following suggestions.

Successful focus groups are guided by a clear objective, involve carefully selected participants, and follow a set of prepared questions and topics. They are ideally supported by one or two moderators and an observer who will take notes or record the discussion and outcomes. If desired and available, use audio or video equipment to record the discussion.

To get the most out of a focus group, carefully consider each of the following aspects.

- *Objective.* Define what you want to record.
- *Participation.*
  - Determine the group size (ideally 10 to 20 participants) and recruit participants (1–2 weeks before the focus group session).
  - Define the composition of your focus group (heterogeneous/homogeneous).
- *Timing and venue.*
  - Schedule the focus group and reserve a location.
  - Call each of the participants the day before the focus group to remind them.
- *Topic.* Create a list of topics that you want to address during the meeting. For a 1.5 hour session, plan to ask five or six questions whose answers will give insight into what you are trying to achieve.
- *Facilitation.* Recruit two moderators, one of whom will take notes. Optionally, recruit an observer to take notes to allow both moderators to focus on the interactions.

- *Technology*. If using recording equipment, set it up and test it and have technical support available in case of malfunctions.
- *Logistics.* Arrange furniture in the room, including any flipcharts or whiteboards; place name-tags; set out refreshments.

Conducting the focus group

Your focus group should follow a predetermined schedule with time allowed for introducing the topic, participants, and methodology. The moderators and (if any) the observer work together to ensure that all questions are addressed, the discussion stays on topic, all participants can contribute, and the schedule is maintained.

The goal of the focus group is to collect useful information, so it is important that participants feel their opinions are valued. Here are key steps for the moderators:

- If using recording equipment, start taping the moment the participants begin to arrive.
- As with the start described above for an interview session (section B.1), welcome the group, introduce yourself as well as the other moderator and observer if present. Start with casual comments to create the right atmosphere and make the group feel as comfortable as possible.
- A moderator provides an overview of the topic, explains how the results of the focus group will be used, and notes that, although the session is being recorded, no names will be used in the final report.
- Make sure each participant signs the informed consent form.
- A moderator outlines the basic rules of the session, such as speak up, don't interrupt each other, switch off mobile phones.
- A moderator asks every participant to introduce him/herself and then starts the questioning.
- Give each individual enough time to respond before opening a group discussion of a question or topic. It is important to hear many viewpoints.
- One moderator (or the observer if used) takes notes, keeps an eye on the time, and checks that all topics are addressed.
- If a topic or issue spurs an unexpected discussion, it is fine to let the group respond as long as the topic is related to the overall objective of the focus group.
- At the end, a moderator summarizes the main points made by the participants, asks for confirmation that the summary is accurate, and thanks everyone for their involvement.
- A moderator hands out the incentives and/or reimbursements.
- After participants have departed, the moderators (and observer if used) should allow themselves time to reflect on questions or insights while the experience is still fresh in their minds.

Analysis

As with most knowledge-capturing methods, gather and review all of the material that was generated by the focus group as soon as possible, ideally the same day. The goal is to generate an analysis of the focus group session that can be shared with colleagues who were not there. The insights obtained from this analysis should be clear and supported by the recording or notes made during the session. Here are some useful steps:

- If the session was recorded electronically, review the recording and your notes. A complete transcript of the recording can provide the basis for later quick review.
- In your report, compare and contrast results by categories of individual focus groups if they are part of a series. Focus groups can be especially helpful if more than one is carried out. The ability to compare and contrast results can serve to confirm what may at first seem like an erroneous insight.
- Use quotes to illustrate your findings.

B.7 Wiki

Wikis are internal or external webpages that allow people to work collaboratively on the same document or collection of documents via a web browser. Wikis can be an effective way to capture knowledge jointly with others. Participants can edit texts, add images and media, and create links between pages. The accessibility of wikis can be restricted.

Advantages

- Most people can create and edit wiki content with minimal guidance.
- Publishing on wikis is usually instantaneous because they do not have a publisher or content gatekeeper.
- Access to confidential documents can be restricted while still allowing the registered group to create and edit them.
- People can work on the same document no matter where they are.
- Wiki software allows reversion to a previous iteration of an article.
- Some wikis allow print versions of wiki articles.
- Many wiki applications come as free open-source software.

Disadvantages

- Wikis need to be managed in order to maintain the desired quality of the content.
- They also need to be managed to keep them well organized, especially when the wiki site becomes very large.

B.8 Collaborative workspace

Collaborative workspace, also called shared workspace or groupware, refers to web-based software that allows group collaboration in a more elaborate or structured way than wikis do. Users can chat, write messages, leave notes, and post images and videos. Some collaborative workspaces are document centered, with users uploading their own documents that other users can comment on, annotate, or discuss online.

Advantages

- » Many different collaborative workspaces exist, with greatly varying functionalities.
- » Most can be configured with the functionalities required by users, and new functionalities can be added when they become necessary.
- » Interaction between people with different types and levels of knowledge can be very beneficial to the organization; collaborative workspaces can become a vehicle for systematic knowledge transfer.
- » They allow for long-term storage of knowledge objects in the form of documents, discussions, and notes that come directly from the participants.

Disadvantages

- » Collaborative workspaces are not very user friendly.
- » They often require substantial induction and a basic level of digital literacy.
- » Participants with lesser communication or foreign language skills at times feel excluded and may drop out.
- » They require active moderation, which may deter some participants.

B.9 Webinar

Web-based conferencing tools allow many participants to share a combination of video, audio, and text presentations at the same time no matter where they are (as long as they have a web connection). Webinars are widely used for meetings, discussions, presentations, lectures, and training events.

Advantages

- » Conferencing tools are often based on show-and-tell principles. They require little skill or effort from the participants, which makes them highly accessible.
- » They appeal to different learning styles (aural, visual, textual).
- » They allow for real-time collaboration across large distances.
- » They can be an important replacement for face-to-face meetings, and thus a cost saver.
- » They make exchanges less formal than physical conferences.

Disadvantages

- » Most web conferencing services are expensive. Free services are usually limited in functionality or capacity.
- » They require good Internet connectivity and special hardware.
- » The quality can vary greatly depending on the Internet connection. Disturbances are unpredictable.

B.10 Online forum

An online forum allows a community to engage in discussion.

Advantages

- » Forums permit a high degree of flexibility. They are accessible at any time and from any place as long as an Internet connection is available.
- » They allow users to express themselves freely in targeted discussion. They encourage equality between users as every message is equally weighted.
- » Forums encourage expression of differing views and opinions on predefined topics.
- » They can feature high-quality discussions as users have time to reflect about and research the topic/comment at hand.
- » They can lead to formation of more sustainable online communities around topics of interest.

Disadvantages

- » Public and unmoderated forums are subject to abuse.
- » Forums are heavily text-based and not very suitable for audio and video.
- » Non-native language speakers may feel less comfortable participating in discussions.
- » They are often heavily dependent on the moderator or certain contributors. It may take a lot of effort from a moderator or resource person to keep the participants engaged in discussion.

B.11 Community of practice

A community of practice (CoP) organizes practitioners or experts in a specific area. CoP offer the possibility to document knowledge through the process of experience sharing amongst people that share a common interest. Participants engage with each other in a process of collective peer learning. In order to support knowledge creation and sharing, the community of practice should ideally be structured around a learning goal. Communities of practice often facilitate various knowledge-sharing interactions, such as chat, forum, discussion, and conferencing. The interactions can be conducted online as well as in person.

Advantages

- » Communities of practice provide a space for people coming together based on a common interest or expertise.

- » Online communities of practice enable members to read, submit, and receive advice and feedback from the community based on questions they may post.
- » Depending on the level of participation, from strictly receptive to highly interactive, participants can gain knowledge and skills from the more experienced members of the community.
- » CoPs can be beneficial to beginners, who are eager to learn from experienced colleagues, but peer learning amongst specialists is equally possible.
- » They allow participants to be involved at their preferred time and place.
- » They maintain resources, ideas, and discussions and in that way create an archive of expertise for a particular technical domain.
- » The knowledge of the group helps support individual professional practitioners, often resulting in a sense of community.

Disadvantages

- » If the community is set up online, the technological aspect can be challenging for less digitally literate participants.
- » It may take a lot of effort to create an effective sense of community for online CoPs. The lack of visual and emotional signals such as body language can make it difficult to encourage meaningful interaction.
- » Users may feel excluded or disconnected without proactive community building or moderation.
- » Participants may be overwhelmed if not carefully introduced into the community, or they may remain passive because of lack of stimulation.
- » CoPs may require intensive moderation to connect knowledge seekers and contributors to each other.
- » Communities of practice can evolve too fast or change direction in a way that members can't keep up with, resulting in a drop in activity.

C. Capturing with Video

You can capture knowledge by just writing down experts' and stakeholders' insights with pen and paper. However, adding audiovisual material can enrich a written record and make it more memorable.

While mastering very elaborate audiovisual tools may not always be an option, neither will it be necessary in most cases. Small digital video cameras record excellent footage (if you have a tape-based camera, consider upgrading to an affordable chip-based digital camera for its greater convenience). Even most smartphones have a decent camera that allows for recording video of an interview or a critical event—if used in the right way, you will be surprised at how good the image is. If using a small video camera or smartphone, you will need to give some special attention to the sound quality. Regardless of the equipment you use, follow these recommendations for optimal audiovisual results.

C.1 The sound

Choose a quiet environment for the recording

Good sound is usually more important than good video, especially when you are interviewing people or recording discussions and presentations. Carefully choose where you will record: Make sure that it is very quiet and that you will not be disturbed. Avoid background noise as much as possible: close windows and doors and if possible turn off audible air conditioning.

Use an external microphone

The built-in microphones on smartphones and affordable video cameras tend to capture a lot of background noise. For better sound, plug an external microphone into your recording device and place it close to your subject.

Earbuds can serve as an external microphone if you are recording one person: plug the earbud/microphone cord into your camera or smartphone and attach the earbud itself to the interviewee's shirt with a paperclip. You will still be far enough away to properly frame the image, and the sound will almost always be crisper than with a microphone that is in the camera itself.

In any case, check the quality of sound on location by plugging a headset or earbuds into your device and play back a test recording; you may find you need to take extra measures or change location to get acceptable sound.

C.2 The image

Pay attention to the camera position

Position the interviewee where light will illuminate your subject's face—if the light comes from behind, your subject will be too dark; and avoid backgrounds that will divert the viewer's attention. Check whether your own chosen position is a safe place to stand. For a steady image, support the device: if holding a smartphone, rest your arm against a wall or on a table or chair; if using a camera, put it on a tripod or table if possible.

Fill the frame

Get close enough to fill almost all of the image frame with your subject's head and shoulders without having to zoom in. Standing farther away and zooming-in may provide a fuzzy image when shown on a large screen. Rotating a video camera is generally not helpful.

Record full sentences

Ask open-ended questions to which the interviewee can respond in a meaningful way, and ask the interviewee to respond in full sentences. Remember, the answers are always more important than your questions, which will likely get edited out anyway later on. (More tips and tricks on conducting an interview can be found in appendix section B.1.)

Record in segments

Stop recording after every answer and start again for the next question. Doing so will reduce the amount you have to edit later on.

Take notes as backup during video recording. After a recording session, you may find that the technology failed. Without a written record, you may not be able to recall important insights that you thought were being captured on the recording. So, when making a video recording, have someone take notes. You can do it yourself if you set the camera on a tripod or suitable surface. If you have to hold the camera (typical with a smartphone), have a colleague do the note-taking. Notes of key takeaways will help you remember the essence of the experience and allow you to build a knowledge asset even if the recording fails.

To limit the potential for problems, check the equipment the day before. Make sure the batteries are fully charged and that there is enough memory space for recording. Bring an additional memory chip (or tapes) and spare battery, if applicable, and a charging cord.

Recording checklist

The following checklist addresses organizational, technical, and content aspects of a video interview. Keep it with you before, during, and after the session!

Before the day of the interview	Yes
Be sure the location is comfortable and provides a suitable environment regarding noise, light, and visual backdrop.	
Reconfirm the date, time, and location with the interviewee.	
Be sure you know how you will get to the interview location.	
Have your list of questions ready.	
Know how to use your recording equipment.	
Provide an external microphone.	
Provide headphones to check the quality of the audio recording.	
Provide a tripod or make some other arrangement that will help you to steady the recording equipment.	
Fully charge the camera/smartphone battery.	
Provide a spare battery if applicable and a charging cord.	
Provide enough recording tape or enough free recording space on your phone or memory card.	
Provide a spare memory card if applicable.	

> continued

> continued from the previous page

On the day of the interview	Yes
Arrive at the interview location well in advance to test your equipment and confirm the suitability of the environment.	

Right before the interview	Yes
Remind the interviewee about the objective of the interview.	
Ask the interviewee to answer the questions in full sentences as your questions will get edited out.	
Ask the interviewee to answer the question concisely at first (the "short answer," but still in complete sentences) before elaborating further.	
Write down the correct spelling of the name and title of the interviewee. Tip: take a close-up shot of his/her business card.	

During the interview	Yes
Have notes taken of key points to allow reconstruction of the interview in case the recording was faulty or becomes lost.	
Start and stop recording for each question to create individual clips, which makes editing easier.	
Check frequently that your equipment is working properly (and that you remembered to press the "record" button). With frequent checking, only one or two questions need to be redone (this may be your only chance to get answers!) when the problem is fixed.	
Follow up on questions for which answers do not seem adequate, raise an or suggest an opportunity for a new knowledge asset.	

At the end of the interview	Yes
Thank the interviewee.	
Ask the interviewee to share any visual resources that would help illustrate the answers, such as pictures, maps, and news articles. Tip: the interviewee may also be able to help if you decide to try filming the location of the experience being reported or interviewing witnesses, if appropriate.	

After the interview	Yes
Listen again to all the answers and identify any potential knowledge gaps.	
Take any necessary remediation to fill knowledge gaps, possibly calling the interviewee for clarifications or scheduling another interview.	
Edit any segments with more than one question and answer into separate clips.	
Remove irrelevant material from each clip.	
Apply any available editing tools to correct sound or lighting problems.	

D. Examples of Knowledge Assets

» Indonesia's National Disaster Management Authority (BNPB)
» Nigeria's Lagos Metropolitan Area Transport Authority (LAMATA)
» Swachh Bharat ("Clean India") Mission (SBM)

D.1 Knowledge Asset from Indonesia's National Disaster Management Authority (BNPB)

Tutoring for Students in Refugee Shelters:
The Experience of Karo District During the Sinabung Eruption in 2014

Executive summary

After the eruption of Mount Sinabung in 2014, affected residents left their homes and had to live in refugee shelters, including school-age children. Coincidentally, the eruption occurred at the time of national exam (UN) for junior and senior high schools' senior classes. The Provincial Government of North Sumatera took the initiative to provide tutoring to prepare these children for the exam. Because the number of local teachers were limited, the government sought assistance from universities. With this, students were able to catch up with their study materials for the national exam.

Context and challenges

» The eruption of Sinabung forced 2,743 school-aged children to live in shelters.

» Initially, the children could not immediately continue their education. It took time to find schools that could take them in.

» Three months before the national exam (UN), the senior class students from junior and senior high schools needed to catch up on their studies so that they would be able to take the exam and pass with good grades. Thus, they needed tutoring.

» The Indonesian President at the time specifically reminded local officials of the importance of education for these young refugees.

» The biggest challenge for the Education Office of Karo Regency was how to manage tutoring for these refugees with only a limited number of teachers at their disposal.

Solution and actions taken

» The Governor of North Sumatera called for a meeting at Merdeka Park, an open space near the Governor's Office frequently used for various government and public activities, such as sporting competitions, youth activities, etc. That meeting was held with various officials from municipal and regency agencies as well as local universities and discussed how the government could manage issues caused by Sinabung eruption, and, in this case, issues related to education.

» The Governor conveyed the importance of tutoring for final year's junior and senior high school students and assigned the University of North Sumatera (USU) and State University of Medan (Unimed) to supply the human resources. USU would conduct

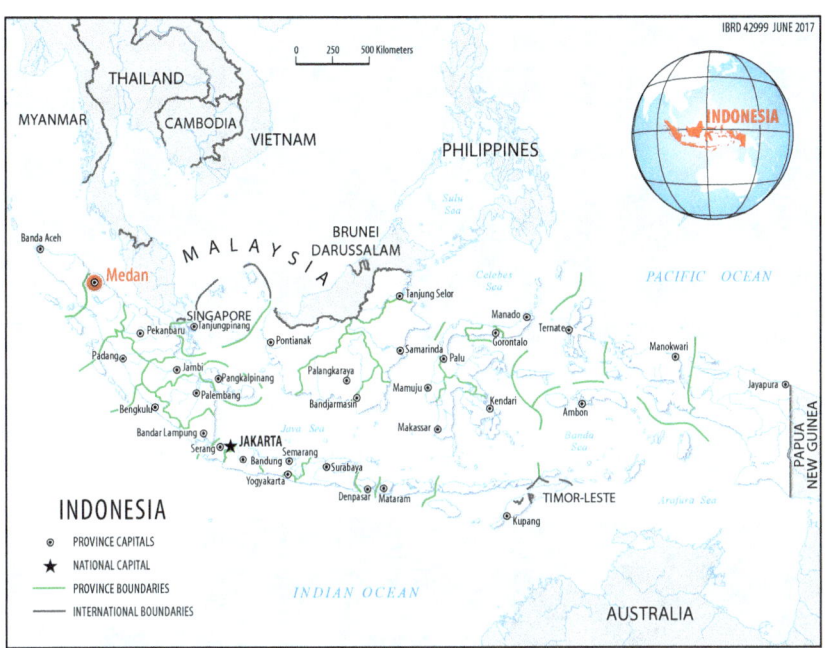

tutoring for senior high school students, while Unimed would tutor the junior high students.

» USU and Unimed then coordinated with the National Task Force for Sinabung Eruption 2014 (Satgas) to prepare the tutoring.

» The task force and the Education Office of Karo Regency conducted student registration in 42 refugee shelters.

» USU and Unimed formed a Teaching Volunteer Team comprising professors and senior year [USU] students with relevant educational background [and provided them] with the test materials.

   » For Junior high: Indonesian language, English, Mathematics, and Science

   » For Senior high: Indonesian, English, Mathematics, Physics, Chemistry, Civics, and Economics

» Tutoring was conducted for two months, twice a week every Saturday and Sunday.

» The task force and Education Office of Karo Regency established the tutoring location based on the shortest distance from the shelter and the availability of necessary facilities.

The tutoring activities

Source: State University of Medan

Results

» A tutoring team of 100 senior year USU students and 24 Unimed lecturers was established.

Source: USU

Source: Unimed

» The tutoring program was conducted in 7 different locations for 483 junior high and 208 senior high students:

Tutoring Location		Students
Junior High level		
SDN Tanjung	Losd Tj Mbelang, Tj Pulo, GBKP Tj Mbelang	147
SMP 1 Tigabinanga	Losd Tigabinanga and Perbesi	68
Mess Provsu L. Gumba	Lau Gumba, Sempajaya, Berastagi, Tongkoh, Korpri	70
Yonif 125/S K.Jahe	25 Kabanjahe shelter posts	198
Senior High level		
Yonif 125/S.K Jahe	25 Kabanjahe shelter posts	87
SMA 1 Tigabinanga	Losd Tigabinanga dan Perbesi	36
SDN Jandi Meriah	Losd Tj Mbelang, Tj Pulo, GBKP Tj Mbelang	85

- » Tutors were dispatched to the 7 locations. The number of tutors was adequate for the whole 2 months of tutoring beginning in February 2014.
- » Based on reports from the national task force, all the final year students who attended this tutoring passed the 2014 national exam with good grades.

Lessons learned

- » Teaching activities during post-disaster response in the shelters was an excellent opportunity to fulfill children's educational needs, especially in facing national exam required for graduation.
- » Cooperation with universities supported teaching activities in post-disaster conditions.

Recommendations

- » Cooperation between local government's education office and local universities is needed to provide effective tutoring program.
- » Continuing school curriculum during time of refuge should be included in shelter management, especially in long-term evacuation periods.

D.2 Knowledge Asset from the Lagos Metropolitan Area Transport Authority (LAMATA)

Conflicts Experienced on the BRT Corridor between Passengers and Ticketers, and Their Resolution

Executive summary

The BRT (Bus Rapid Transport) scheme was introduced by LAMATA to the travelling public of Lagos State in March 2008 to, amongst other reasons, offer a more efficient, reliable, safe, timely and cost effective means of commuting on the Mile 12-TBS Corridor.

The project has witnessed wide acceptance and patronage since its Inception; it has also been exposed to some challenges which affect different aspects of the operations. One of such challenges that this paper addresses is that of conflicts that exists between Passengers and Ticket Vendors (Ticketers).

Of interest to us are conflicts arising from:

1. Overriding tendencies of some passengers
2. Insufficient change during ticket purchase
3. Ticketers getting edgy as a result of work stress

Context and challenge

Conflicts on the BRT corridor between Passengers and Ticketers have posed a nagging challenge since the inception of the scheme; the situation sometimes degenerates to physical exchanges between the two major stakeholders.

Before the advent of the BRT, the major mode of transportation was the yellow buses known as danfo, and their alternative to having Ticketers were bus conductors; these bus conductors were notorious for being extremely abusive, indifferent and vitriolic as a result of their constant repeated exposure to passengers who exhibited attitudes of rudeness. This occurrence was on a daily basis on the road, at bus parks, and garages where the Passengers were encountered; of course, these instances currently occur on the BRT corridor.

The main challenges identified are getting the commuters and Ticketers to transact business in the absence of conflict and reinforce good will. In addition boundaries were not in place as passengers did not have defined and documented rights beyond the verbal contracts entered into. This undocumented contract is breached at will.

This results in hostility and lack of trust shown by both stakeholders which hinders the relationship and creates a negative atmosphere during transactions, which is like a vicious cycle constantly reinforcing negative perceptions on both shareholders.

The consequences both long and short term includes:
- » Loss of profit as a result of lack of patronage by passengers
- » Loss of goodwill
- » Bad image for the regulatory body involved
- » Increase in travel time
- » Loss of man hours

Secondly the issue of overriding was identified as a gimmick used repeatedly by many Passengers to take advantage of the system by demoralizing the checker staff at fadeyi by engaging them in conflict, thus wasting the time of the other passengers who instinctively tended to align themselves with the non-compliant rogue.

Action steps and solutions
- » Considering that the Identified issues can be seen as resulting from communication gaps, solutions to resolving the conflicts are also drawn from actions that encourage better understanding and cooperation between passengers and Ticketers
- » One of such solution is to determine the most frequently asked questions by the commuters which could be drawn up and replicated using media like bulletin boards, flyers, brochures to disseminate this information as opposed to constantly having to do so verbally.
- » Removing that particular responsibility would enable them to focus on the most pressing issues on ground provided the medium selected to communicate such info was applicable/relevant.
- » The culture here is that people would rather tend to respect and uphold, without disputes any printed information. The solution proposed was to print instructions on the back of the tickets as guides to passengers on termination of travel on particular zone
- » In addition a sticker showing the same information should be pasted at different bus stops where passengers could easily read the notices and have them referred to by the checkers to discourage rogue attitudes with passengers.
- » On the issue of lack of change caused by passengers presenting higher denomination thus creating delays and bottlenecks was to be dealt with by notifying the passengers through the use of various media platforms that the management would not accept bad note and passengers were to bear the responsibility for having exact fares.

Lessons learned
- » Passengers are more Inclined to adhere to printed communication
- » Having exact fares reduces conflicts and saves travel time
- » Printed information reduces burden of passenger surge on Ticket Vendors
- » Periodic training for Ticket Vendors

D.3 Knowledge Asset from India's Swachh Bharat ("Clean India") Mission (SBM)

"War Room": Bijnor District Adopts a Novel Way to Monitor Sanitation

Context and key challenge

Ever since the Swachh Bharat Mission was launched in October 2014, frantic efforts are on in states and districts all across India to become Open Defecation Free (ODF). But monitoring the quality and design of toilets, sustained behavior change and toilet usage continues to be a challenge for the government at national, state and district levels.

"The Sanitation Mission requires a large army of foot soldiers in every village, both government and non-government functionaries and Nigrani (Monitoring) Committees to do behavior change. To monitor, train and have an incentive structure in place for this army, we needed a command center to wage this war against poor sanitation and hygiene. The trainers are using Gandhian tools and methods and we needed this 24/7 communication mechanism to enable interaction between district, block, village level committees and stakeholders to help them solve the sanitation challenge."

—**Vijay Kiran Anand, Mission Director, Swachh Bharat Mission Gramin (Rural), UP**

Solution

Bijnor District in western Uttar Pradesh (UP), which has run a dynamic ODF campaign, has come up with one possible answer—a unique innovation and institutional mechanism called the **"War Room."** Started in April 2016, it was the original brainchild of current Swachh Bharat Mission—Gramin (SBMG) Director of UP, formerly District Magistrate Bijnor. The current Bijnor administration relies on computer data entry operators, support staff and CLTS trainers across the district, who work round the clock in «mission mode,» **to hold all their SBMG workers accountable, targeting genuinely needy beneficiaries, help catalyze and monitor community behavior change and even "monitor monitoring groups" themselves.**

With 11 Blocks in the District, some very far from District headquarters, an increasing work load of field level activities and data generation, Bijnor District Administration felt the need to open an ODF War Room to create a centralized tracking system. They wanted to understand what triggering activities were taking place in the field, challenges being faced in the ground, where improvements are required, where the teams are going, are they getting support or not, are the officers attached the teams doing their duties properly or not and other important related aspects of the ODF work on the ground.

Although the concept may be borrowed from and inspired by political campaigns, Bijnor District has been the first district to successfully adapt it to a government scheme for its SBMG effort and invested time, resources and money to ensure its meaningful use as a monitoring mechanism.

a | Functions of the War Room

The War Room is located in the District Administration office itself, where all the officials sit right from the District Magistrate (DM) and Chief Development Officer (CDO) to the building guards. The **benefit of this is proximity to decision makers, ease of addressing technical and other challenges and the ability to "watch over" the War Room itself, making the monitoring objective multi-layered and full proof,** to the extent possible.

"The concept of the War Room was to connect it to computers, internet and Whatsapp groups. Our trainers would go in the field for a 5-day triggering programme in each Gram Panchayat (GP) and take photographic evidence of their work and sent it to the War Room every day. So, by just sitting in one place, we get the picture of the entire District. Slowly, it became very popular and now we are doing many things through the War Room and it has been very advantageous for us."

—Jagat Raj, District Magistrate, Bijnor

The War Room **performs three main monitoring and data-entry related** functions to assist Bijnor's District Administration with its SBMG campaign.

> "To do total tracking for the entire day and to do it in a time-bound manner, we took the concept of the War Room. And this concept we have seen being used in many democratic systems to communicate your message to the public. The concept even exists in the political campaigns. So, to take your message to the community and to bring the community's messages to the administration, plus to include our champions in the work and to track their work, we took on this innovation."
>
> **—Indramani Tripathy, Chief Development Officer, Bijnor District**

First, it **helps to monitor behaviour change progress across the entire district from just one room and keep its own SBMG trainers and field level officers accountable**—The administration's CLTS trainers span out in each Gram Panchayat (small cluster of villages), join up with there with community level monitoring groups called "Nigrani Committees"—men, women and children of the village who volunteer or are nominated to check open defecation in the village. CLTS trainers both trigger behaviour change and monitor it with Nigrani Committees and have to send photographic proof of these activities to the War Room, every morning and evening through WhatsApp. These images are then fed into the computers in the War Room by the data entry operators for each Block. "Trackers" in the War Room take daily attendance of CLTS trainers at 4 a.m. every morning. In this way, the War Room "monitors monitoring groups."

Second, the War Room **enables the District Administration to carry out its other innovative idea of "Compressed Demand" successfully.** Under the concept, **only the genuinely needy and very poor are chosen in their baseline of target beneficiaries who require government assistance to build toilets through the financial incentive.** For each GP, the 'Compressed Demand" baseline is arrived at by the CLTS trainers during their 5-day residential triggering schedule through a door-to-door survey. They compile the list and send it to the War Room every Friday. Another verification of the list does takes place at the GP level, changes are made if required and finally, the data entry operators feed the information directly into an App on the national SBMG website, as required.

Third, the War Room **is utilized to address any other data related requirements and requests of sanitation work for the district administration** to ensure that information its district information remains updated and correct on the SBMG national website. For instance, shifting of beneficiary information within a Block or updating beneficiary progress information on the SBMG website App.

Based on the above three main functions, the War Room provides the district sanitation progress and data to the administrative leadership—District Magistrate, Chief Development Officer and District Panchayati Raj Officer. Among the monitoring indicators on which the War Room reports to the administration include daily progress report of toilets constructed per revenue village and weekly report of CLTS trainers performance/visits, summary report of MIS feeding and photo uploading, reporting of baseline update status and performance of Nigrani (Monitoring) Committees.

b | Structure—Three theatres of the War Room

The first theatre is **District level War Room** itself, where **four "trackers"** work in shifts from 4 a.m. until 8:30pm to take daily morning and evening attendance of the CLTS trainers in the field and receive and check photographic proof of their morning and evening triggering and monitoring activities via Whatsapp. At 10 am, the **11 computer data entry operators**—one for each Block in Bijnor—enter information on computers of the attendance, photographic proof and spend the rest of the day until 6pm, entering household sanitation data of beneficiaries with completed toilets based on "compressed demand" directly into the national SBMG website—a requirement under the scheme.

The second theatre is smaller level **Block level "War Rooms,"** which were created in June 2016. They have **field level workers who are familiar with computers** reporting to the Block Development Officer (BDO) and **2 Block level motivators** each. Their purpose is to allow the administration to gauge in each Block where have toilets been built, where is triggering team facing challenges, where do they need support, providing information required for district level War Room, addressing delays in compressed demand list receipt and uploading photos of completed toilets. The Block level and District level War Rooms remain in daily contact and coordination.

"Ever since the War Room has opened up, I feel that we are achieving greater success each passing day because there is passion among the people. When I open the War Room at 4 a.m. every morning and take attendance of our field trainers, they tell us that they feel so good about what they are doing that it is benefitting their health and allowing them to do public service."

—Rakesh, Tracker, War Room, Bijnor District

The third theatre of the War Room is are the **Gram Panchayats where the CLTS trainers do triggering work,** monitor behavior change and conduct the door-to-door survey to make a baseline of "compressed demand" of eligible and needy beneficiaries. The trainers stay in the GPs and immerse themselves in the community for 5 days and **submit an activity report every week to the War Room and the "compressed demand" baseline list.**

c | Challenges in set up

Even a visionary and dynamic effort is not without its challenges and the War Room has its share. Perhaps the biggest challenge the administration faced was in getting staff to do work in addition to their normal official duties, put in long and late hours. To have a routine of waking up at 3 a.m. every morning is tough and tiring for anyone. The administration was fortunate to get highly passionate and dedicated people.

They also had to train everyone for everything from a start and to make them capable for achieving their purpose with 100% commitment.

Another big challenge has been with internet connectivity, which often slows down or is lost completely. This problem impacts the data entry operators the most, whose painstaking work can often be made more difficult when the national SBMGwebsite is running slow due to an overload or showing repeated error messages upon submission of data.

d | Sustainability

One of the ways in which the Bijnor Administration has institutionalized and sustains the War Room is to **actually invest in the basic infrastructure and resources required** to run it successfully. For initial investment, the Bijnor Administration choose an appropriate unused room in their District Office and the efficiently used computers that are given to each GP by the State government, which were not being used.

> "Suppose someone leaves or gets transferred, all the information recorded in the War Room will be part of institutional memory and documented record of the District and its ODF work. Second, if someone wants to access it later, the War Room serves as an 'online ODF library' for Bijnor for the future."
>
> —**Manish Kumar, District Panchayati Raj Officer, Bijnor**

The War Room was thus outfitted with 11 computers and work stations for 11 data entry operators— one dedicated person for each of the 11 Blocks in Bijnor, who are paid as per the SBMG guidelines. They were recruited from existing Block level resources. There are 4 support staff drawn from the government existing salaried staff. They rotate as "trackers" in shifts from 4 a.m. in the morning until 8:30pm in the evening every day. Another important investment is an internet broadband connection and since the War Room is located in the District Headquarters itself, it is easily linked to a printer, photocopier and scanner and a telephone line.

In order to create almost **"airtight" accountability in the whole system,** the DPRO of Bijnor took the initiative to install another layer of monitoring of the "War Room" itself from his office through a camera monitoring (CCTV) system linked to an intercom and his own mobile phone—from the mobile phone, he can monitor everything going on in the War Room whether he is in the office or not and from the intercom, he has a "hotline" to the War Room directly from his office to keep an eye on them or to cater to time-sensitive requests.

To address the challenges of personnel, Bijnor Administration hired support staff as "trackers" in the War Room who were willing to go beyond the call of duty and put in extra hours. They introduced shifts or rotation between "trackers" to ensure nobody gets burned out. To keep motivation levels up, the Administration introduced a small monetary incentive each month for the data entry operators and give out awards on key milestone achievements. Since Bijnor hired new staff in the War Room and had to train them from a start,

they checked the eligibility, computer proficiency and capabilities of data entry operators, including Microsoft Word and Excel skills. To address the internet connectivity challenge, they have taken two internet lines. In the main office, there is a wireless internet connection and in the War Room, it is the lease line connection. So, sometimes, when it the internet breaks down in the War Room, they take back-up connection from the main office.

"If I want to contact 100 people, then if I talk to everyone, then I need 100 minutes. But if I do it through the War Room, it will take me at most 10-15 minutes. Also, helps us to prioritize work. It shakes us up and reminds us that you have work to do."

—**Manish Kumar, District Panchayati Raj Officer, Bijnor**

Results

This "out of the box" thinking, borrowing simple, creative concepts and applying them to Bijnor's SBMG work and the dedication to execute well has paid some rich dividends for the district. As of March 2017, Bijnor has reached almost **80 % coverage of toilets** and usage in their district compared in less than a year. The **"Compressed Demand"** concept that is facilitated through the **War Room**'s tracking and data-entry efforts has not only reduced the number of toilets

> *"We first heard this concept of War Room from Bijnor only. The value is that earlier if someone used to come, people had to wander about everywhere to find out about SBMG work and data in our district—baseline survey information, which are the eligible GPs, who is the Gram Pradhan or Sachiv in a particular Gram Panchayat. If the common man or even SBMG worker wanted information, they got lost. Now they contact the Block level or District level war rooms for information directly. They've got to know what ODF really is because of this ODF War Room. Second, monitoring is now properly possible—of triggering activities, toilet construction and behavior change, Nigrani (Monitoring) Committees and training."*
>
> **—Anamika Tripathy, District Project Consultant, Swachh Bharat Mission, Varanasi District**

needed by 1 lakh, it has also saved the government almost INR 120 crores or USD 1.2 billion. On March 29, 2017, less than a year after the War Room was opened, they celebrated **crossing the 1 lakh mark for entering beneficiary data** in the national SBMG website with a cake-cutting ceremony and gave awards to the War Room data entry operators and staff.

A **systematic way and institutional mechanism to monitor and follow-up has been established** so that nothing falls through the cracks. At the field level, the triggering team that is going into the field are using the concept of the War Room to **deepen the CLTS engagement** on the ground and also **activating Nigrani (community level monitoring) committees.** On the administrative front, the thinking of the administrative officials can be quickly conveyed through such a set up to the field and the Challenges from the field come through the War Room as a conduit to the Administration through monitoring of activities. The entire line of communication has been strengthened through War Room from District to GP and GP to District. There have been important efficiency savings through the War Room and they have made a "centralized system to decentralize" the sanitation work.

Other district government departments in Bijnor itself, such as health, education and women and child welfare have already started **replicating the War Room** for their own purposes and delivering results such as **better attendance of teachers and doctors/nurses/staff in schools and clinics,** respectively. The state government issued an order to all districts in UP to establish a War Room for their ODF work. Many **other districts in UP,** inspired by Bijnor's innovation, are **replicating the War Room** to varying degrees including Varanasi, Agra, Shamli, Pratapgarh, Mirzapur, Amroha and Ferozabad.

Lessons learned

The administration identified a few main areas where they learned lessons as a result of the War Room innovation. First, through the field level **monitoring** and tracking, they were able to see where they were going wrong in some cases with **toilet design** and were able to make improvements. Second, they have learned lessons and gained insights on how to make ODF work more sustainable. For instance, the administration is already thinking on many fronts on how **to utilize the War Room for ODF plus or Solid Liquid Waste Management (SLWM) work.** Future steps may include video conferencing between District and Block level war rooms, utilizing the War Room for ODF verification and documentation and **also to monitor toilet usage through "Swacchta Sangrahis"—committed volunteers** at the Gram Panchayat level who will be appointed to check "slippage" i.e. people who slip back into open defecation.

Recommendations

A proposal to scale-up the War Room concept with requisite resources across UP districts, other states and even in the sanitation mission office at national level, has been made by the current SBMG (UP) Mission Director to Ministry of Drinking Water and Sanitation and is under consideration. If undertaken, the scale-up and expansion will happen at all levels including in the functions of War Rooms, which could include **concurrent monitoring of CLTS activities** with respect to the ODF campaign, submission of demand received from Gram Panchayats and Blocks for **payouts to finance any outstanding dues** to beneficiaries after due diligence, monitoring of **district level verification procedure** of ODF status, **resolution of disputes** in the field by escalating to the right person, **identifying needs for training and capacity building** of stakeholders and **monitoring the IEC (communication) schedule** and events of districts and **associated costs.** Some of these functions are already taking place to varying degrees through Bijnor's War Room mechanism but if the proposal is accepted, these additional functions can be formalized with provision for required resources to carry such tasks out effectively.

For now, the War Room is helping "Bemisaal (unmatched) Bijnor" to keep a fire burning among its trainers, staff and community alike for public service through external monitoring pressure and steady internal behavior change.

E. Functions and Terms of Reference

1. Knowledge-Sharing Steering Committee
2. Knowledge-Management/Knowledge-Sharing Coordination Team
3. Chief Knowledge and Learning Officer
4. Knowledge and Learning Specialist
5. Knowledge-Capturing Specialist
6. Audiovisual Media Specialist

E.1. Knowledge-Sharing Steering Committee

Description

This document sets the Terms of Reference for [Your Organization's] Knowledge-Sharing Steering Committee. The Terms of Reference establish the Steering Committee's mission, objectives, membership, and operational procedures. The Knowledge-Sharing Steering Committee is the governing body for guiding the development, implementation, and continuous improvement of [Your Organization's] knowledge-sharing initiatives, policies, and strategy.

(Use this section to provide background information related to the establishment of the Steering Committee, its mission, and objectives. This will include decisions made regarding knowledge sharing in your organization, relevant events, related organizational structures and hierarchies, and the process behind the establishment of the committee.)

Responsibilities

- Devising a strategy for knowledge sharing
- Supervising the knowledge sharing change process
- Creating a broad, organization-wide awareness of the policies, perspectives, and goals associated with all knowledge sharing activities
- Ensuring that the roles and responsibilities for the performance of the knowledge-sharing programs are clear and complementary
- Fostering communications and cooperation across business units and departments for knowledge-sharing programs, policies, and activities and ensuring alignment of operational units with support functions in their implementation of knowledge sharing
- Establish performance measures and metrics for the organization's knowledge-sharing activities
- Appointing an implementation team and its leader
- Approving knowledge-sharing partnerships

» Supporting and regularly briefing senior management on all knowledge-sharing issues

(Use this section to describe the specific roles and responsibilities of the Knowledge Sharing Steering Committee members. This will include the activities that they will be accountable for, what their commitments are and the expectations of each member of the Knowledge-Sharing Steering Committee.)

Qualifications/Membership

(Use this section to list the members of the Knowledge-Sharing Steering Committee; include title as well as role within the team.)

Operations/Frequency of Meetings

(Use this section to establish the frequency of the Steering Committee's meetings and how these are to be conducted. Include how the decisions and minutes will be shared with staff.)

E.2 Knowledge-management/Knowledge-sharing coordination team

Description

This document sets the Terms of Reference for [Your Organization's] Knowledge-Management Coordination Team. The Terms of Reference establishes the Team's mission, objectives, membership and operational procedures. The Knowledge-Management Coordination Team is the implementing body for knowledge sharing initiatives, policies and strategy. The team is composed of knowledge and learning specialists and representatives from all operational and administrative departments of the organization. The team is in charge of implementation of major knowledge-sharing programs and activities in your organization; relevant events, platforms, and systems; development of knowledge and learning products and offerings; and other activities as they relate to the knowledge-sharing strategy framework. It further monitors the organization's knowledge-sharing activities and feeds performance reports back to the Knowledge-Sharing Steering Committee.

(Use this section to provide any relevant background information related to the establishment of the team, its mission, and objectives.)

Responsibilities

» Implementation of the knowledge sharing strategy

» Development of knowledge sharing related budgets

» Monitoring of knowledge sharing related expenses

» Coordination and organization of organization-wide and cross-departmental knowledge sharing activities and events

» Coordination of knowledge-capturing efforts in the departments

» Proactive development of innovative internal and external knowledge sharing activities

» Ensuring quality control and timely validation of knowledge assets

- » Coordination of the development of high quality knowledge and learning products
- » Coordination of the design and implementation of high quality learning offerings
- » Implementation and maintenance of knowledge sharing systems and platforms
- » Design, implementation and management of communities of practice and knowledge sharing networks
- » Coordination of knowledge sharing related monitoring & evaluation and reporting efforts
- » Development of communications on knowledge sharing related activities
- » Implementation and active use of collaborations and partnerships as they relate to knowledge sharing and peer learning, including identification of outsourcing partners
- » Day-to-day liaison with domestic and international partners on knowledge sharing activities

(Use this section to describe the specific roles and responsibilities of the Knowledge Management Coordination Team members. This will include the activities that they will be accountable for, what their commitments are and the expectations of each team member.)

Qualifications/Membership

(Use this section to list each member of the Knowledge-Management Coordination Team; include title as well as role within the team.)

Operations/Frequency of Meetings

(Use this section to establish the frequency of the Knowledge-Management Coordination Team's meetings and how they are to be conducted. Include how decisions and minutes will be shared with staff.)

E.3 Chief knowledge and learning officer (CKO/CLO)

Job description

The Chief Knowledge and Learning Officer is part of the senior management team of the organization and oversees the design and implementation of the organization's knowledge management and learning strategies. The CKO/CLO develops efficiencies in the knowledge value chain by creating an enabling environment that is conducive to systematic knowledge sharing and organizational learning. He/she is overseeing the implementation of a knowledge infrastructure that supports informed decision making and continuous learning to prepare management and staff to deliver on their operational tasks in the most effective manner.

Responsibilities

- » Oversee the development and implementation of a knowledge management strategy/framework/policies for the organization

- » Oversee the development of functions, systems, tools and processes that make use of knowledge to improve organizational effectiveness
- » Actively promote the use of knowledge and learning within and outside the organization
- » Role model exemplary knowledge sharing behavior to colleagues and partners of the organization
- » Identify, promote and use knowledge and learning partnerships that support and enrich knowledge management and sharing within and beyond the organization
- » Encourage knowledge capturing and sharing throughout the organization
- » Design and implement incentive mechanisms to reward exemplary knowledge capturing and sharing behavior
- » Design and implement a results framework to monitor and evaluate effectiveness of knowledge and learning related measures

Qualifications

- » A master's degree in knowledge management, instructional design, learning, or a related field and at least 10 years' applied experience in developing, managing, and implementing knowledge-management strategies
- » Experience in organizational change management
- » Excellent collaborative leadership skills
- » Excellent interpersonal and people management skills, including the ability to motivate others
- » Strong strategic-thinking and integration skills, with ability to identify opportunities and obstacles for systematic knowledge capturing and sharing within the organization
- » Sound understanding of technologies, platforms, and IT infrastructure that facilitate knowledge management and sharing
- » Good communication and listening skills

E.4 Knowledge and learning specialist

Job description

The Knowledge and Learning Specialist executes the knowledge and learning strategy of the organization and implements the knowledge and learning activities of the organization/department. The specialist sets up and manages knowledge management and learning systems and administers the infrastructure for systematic capturing, managing, sharing, and finding of information.

Responsibilities

- Helps to foster organization-wide knowledge sharing, so that the organization's know-how, information, and experience is shared inside and, where applicable, outside the organization with partners and other stakeholders
- Gathers and organizes information for the organization's knowledge repository
- Facilitates seamless knowledge sharing across the organization's departments
- Regularly interacts with operations colleagues to ensure continuous capturing, managing, and sharing of critical knowledge in the organization
- Manages the content on the organization's knowledge and learning platforms
- Analyzes the characteristics of existing and emerging technologies and their use for better management and sharing of knowledge
- Develops the taxonomies of the organization's knowledge and learning repositories
- Supports the design of the organization's knowledge and learning platforms and functionalities
- Extracts high-value knowledge assets for dissemination
- Supports the advocating, training, and mainstreaming of knowledge management and learning functions in the organization
- Manages the organization's community-of-practice platforms
- Models active knowledge sharing throughout the organization and with partners

Qualifications

- A bachelor's degree in knowledge management, instructional design, learning or a related field and at least five years' applied experience in setting up and administrating knowledge management and learning systems
- Sound understanding of technologies, platforms, and IT infrastructure that facilitate knowledge management and sharing
- Ability to develop an information architecture and taxonomies to support findability of the organization's knowledge assets
- Good team work and collaboration skills
- Good interpersonal skills and the ability to motivate others to contribute to and make use of the knowledge and learning offerings of the organization
- Good communication and listening skills
- Attention to detail
- Ability to quickly develop a sound understanding of the operational departments' knowledge needs and assets

- » Ability to assess situations quickly and make independent decisions regarding capturing and sharing of knowledge assets
- » Basic understanding of common business processes within the organization as well as with external partners
- » Proactive work ethic

E.5 Knowledge-capturing specialist

Job description

The knowledge-capturing specialist supports the organization-wide knowledge identification, capturing, validation and formatting processes. The specialist extracts and documents valuable experiences and lessons learned from operational and administrative colleagues in the organization. Supports development of a comprehensive, targeted, highly useful knowledge base that allows staff throughout the organization access mission-critical knowledge.

Responsibilities
- » Captures the experiential knowledge of colleagues and experts throughout the organization as well as external stakeholders to populate and grow the organization's repository of valuable and sharable knowledge assets
- » Continuously scans the organization for knowledge that is important for the organization's operations
- » Interviews internal and external stakeholders to extract mission-critical experiences and lessons learned for further scale-up and sharing
- » Manages the logistics, set-up, design, and implementation of synchronous knowledgecapturing activities, including meetings, focus groups, and workshops
- » Designs and manages online capturing activities, including surveys, wikis, blogs, e-discussions
- » Evaluates the usefulness of knowledge to be captured for replication and scale up
- » Edits the knowledge assets in regards to language, formatting and content
- » Analyzes, synthesizes, and summarizes the captured knowledge and transforms it into formatted knowledge assets that are of high quality, standardized and sharable
- » Uses audiovisual tools to capture knowledge at high quality
- » Populates the attributes and qualifiers of knowledge assets to ensure good findability
- » Develops trusted relationships with a variety of stakeholders within and outside the organization

Qualifications

- An advanced degree in journalism, English, knowledge management, or a related field and at least five years' applied experience in journalism
- Excellent interview skills to ensure optimal documentation and extraction of knowledge derived from personal experiences
- Excellent journalistic skills
- Objectivity to identify and collect experiences that are deemed worth sharing
- Profound interest and curiosity in the processes that make up the professional activities in the organization
- Sound understanding of the professional environment and activities of the organization as well as of skills and competencies required to carry out the technical function within the organization
- Motivation to share knowledge, successful practices, and lessons learned and interest in improving the effectiveness of the organization
- Altruistic attitude and willingness to share knowledge
- Sound time-management skills to adequately balance operational and knowledge work
- Ability to objectively assess and analyze the skills, competencies, and expertise of co-workers
- Ability and self-discipline to systematically reflect on past assignments to continuously improve
- Ability to apply capturing activities such as interviews, observations, and group discussions
- Writing and media production skills to process captured experiences in a way that they can be communicated or disseminated. This may include basic media and digital literacy skills
- Ability to digest information and analyze, synthesize, and summarize it in clear and concise ways
- Listening and observing skills to pick up events, facts, behaviors, and activities
- Ability to ask relevant questions
- Good interpersonal communication skills to relate with a variety of stakeholders, including senior colleagues
- Emotional capacity and empathy to connect with others and to build trust
- Typing and note-taking skills
- Good facilitation skills to be able to tease out knowledge and information from other people
- Familiarity with IT tools for producing knowledge materials

B.6 Audiovisual media specialist

Job description

The Audiovisual Media Specialist supports the capturing and recording of experiences and lessons learned throughout and beyond the organization. The specialist manages all technical logistics, including for location set-up, audio, lighting, and audiovisual (AV) equipment to ensure a smooth recording process. The AV Media Specialist also supports the development of AV-based learning offerings and ensures knowledge assets and products are professionally edited.

Responsibilities

- Records interviews and other knowledge extraction activities using AV equipment
- Professionally edits AV recordings for further use in knowledge assets and more comprehensive knowledge and learning products
- Supports the knowledge-capturing specialist with all technology-based tools and processes
- Helps locate and maintain a technically suitable environment in which the recording will take place

Qualifications

- A bachelor's degree in audiovisual media, multimedia design, videography, or a related field and at least five years' applied experience as a cameraman and/or video editor
- Excellent understanding of AV equipment and recording options available to ensure good quality knowledge capturing
- Excellent audio and video editing skills with a good grasp of AV editing technologies and tools
- Good communication skills
- Good interpersonal skills a plus

GLOSSARY

Italicized terms have their own entry.

Content management system (CMS)

Computer application that allows publishing, editing, and modifying content, as well as organizing, deleting, and maintenance, from a central interface. Such systems provide procedures to manage workflow in a collaborative environment. CMSs are often used to run websites containing blogs and news. Many corporate and marketing websites use CMSs, which typically avoid the need for hand coding.

Experiential (or implicit) knowledge

Knowledge that resides in people's heads as intangible knowledge but which can be converted into explicit knowledge through a process of documentation and capturing.

Explicit (or codified) knowledge

Knowledge that has been articulated, codified, stored, and readily transmitted to others. The information contained in textbooks, manuals, documents, procedures, case studies, and how-to videos are examples of explicit knowledge. Polanyi (1966) defines explicit or codified knowledge as "knowledge that can be transmitted by formal systematic language" (cited in Schwandt and Marquardt 1999, 127). In Zack (1999, 46), "explicit knowledge is more precisely and formally articulated, although removed from the original context of creation or use (e.g. an abstract mathematical formula derived from physical experiments)."

Knowledge asset

A digital document or collection of media containing knowledge about a specific question or challenge. Typically short and learner-oriented, a knowledge asset presents key lessons learned from an operational experience and provides decision-making support for one particular challenge. The story it presents follows a standardized format— tracing the problem, actions, results, lessons, and recommendations—that makes the asset a self-contained lesson. It should be validated in a peerreview process and formatted with metadata allowing it to be found within a larger knowledge repository. The model of a knowledge asset is also used in the concept of mental "theories of action," which describes behavior at individual, group, and organizational levels. Similar to the structure of a knowledge asset, a simple theory of action would include a basic description of the context, the problem to be addressed (goal), and a strategy to take action to overcome the problem, assuming conditions are comparable (Argyris and Schön 1974 and 1978).

Knowledge capturing

The process of converting the knowledge or experience that resides in the mind of an individual into an explicit representation, whether in print, electronic, multimedia form.

Knowledge-capturing team

A team that systematically and uniformly document lessons learned from operational experiences that have not yet been explicitly recorded or are difficult to record. Its goal is to capture critical insights and takeaways for potential replication elsewhere. Team members possess an ability to quickly grasp the key challenges and solution paths in a journalistic way. Their most common techniques are interviews and focus groups.

Knowledge-creating organization

An organization that is able to translate tacit knowledge into explicit knowledge applicable to a different context and formalize it. Over time, the new knowledge itself becomes tacit and available to become explicit in yet another context (Nonaka and Takeuchi 1995). To achieve these transformations, managers and staff need to engage in continuous reflection at the individual, team, and organizational levels, and time and space for such reflection needs to be provided.

Knowledge exchange

See Knowledge sharing.

Knowledge hub

An institution or network dedicated to capturing, sharing, and exchanging development experiences with national and international partners to accelerate development (Government of Indonesia and others 2012).

Knowledge management

A discipline promoting an integrated approach to identifying, capturing, evaluating, retrieving, and sharing all of an enterprise's information assets. As defined by the Gartner Group (Duhon 1998), these assets may include databases, documents, policies, procedures, and previously uncaptured expertise and experience in individual workers. It is intended to improve efficiency and the quality of products and services and to achieve innovations. Although knowledge management overlaps with organizational learning, the former may be distinguished by a greater focus on knowledge as a strategic asset and on encouraging knowledge sharing. Knowledge management is an enabler of organizational learning.

Knowledge repository

A data storage system that can comprise multiple, networked technologies. It allows for centralized management of, and provision of access to, knowledge assets and supports resource management to add, maintain, update, recycle, and discard knowledge assets. Knowledge repositories are also referred to as knowledge-management or knowledge-resource platforms.

Knowledge sharing

A subset of knowledge management encompassing the exchange of knowledge (information, skills, experiences, or expertise) within and across organizations. Although it can be one-directional, knowledge sharing in most cases is a two-way or multilateral exchange in which the parties learn from each other. Knowledge sharing is more than mere communication, as much knowledge in organizations is hard to articulate. In development work, some knowledge sharing has a regional aspect. For example, South-South knowledge sharing refers to exchanges among partners and peers across developing countries.

Learning organization

"An organization that is skilled at creating, acquiring, and transferring knowledge and at modifying behavior to reflect new knowledge and insights" (DuBrin 2005, 410). Learning organizations exhibit five main characteristics: personal mastery, mental models, a shared vision, team learning, and—the fifth element that integrates them—systems thinking (Senge 1990).

Organizational behavior

The study of individual and team behavior in an organization, of the interaction between individuals and the organization, and of the organization itself.

Organizational culture

According to DuBrin (2005, 337–39), "a system of shared values and beliefs that influence worker behavior...Often its origin lies in the values, administrative practices, and personality of the founder or founders. Also the leader's vision can have a heavy impact on culture.... Organizational culture responds to and mirrors the conscious and unconscious choices, behavior patterns, and prejudices of top-level managers." DuBrin 2005 posits nine dimensions of organizational culture: values, organizational stories with underlying meanings, myths, degree of stability, resource allocations and rewards, rites and rituals, sense of ownership, belief in a higher purpose, and innovativeness.

Organizational effectiveness

The extent to which an organization delivers on its mandate and fulfills the demand of stakeholders it engages with.

Organizational learning

An area of knowledge within organizational theory that studies the way an organization learns and adapts. It is also defined as "a system of actions, actors, symbols, and processes that enables an organization to transform information into valued knowledge which in turn increases its long-run adaptive capacity" (Schwandt 1993, 8). "Organizational Learning involves making tacit theories of action explicit so that people can become aware of, critically examine, and change them...[It] facilitates accountability by increasing self-awareness and enhancing the ability to exercise conscious choice and intention" (Lipshitz, Friedman, and Popper 2007, 122). To increase the organization's readiness one must develop the capability to learn how to learn. Policy, structures and skills are needed to do so (Schön 1975).

Organizational memory

Shared interpretations of an organization's past as related by the members of the organization. Organizational memory can be "episodic" or "semantic." The former describes memories of a person who had the experiences contained in the memories, whereas the latter is independent of those experiences—for example, through retelling of stories by someone who was not part of an actual experience (Schwandt and Marquardt 1999, 206).

Tacit knowledge

The knowledge in people's heads. Tacit knowledge is personal, context-specific, and therefore hard to formalize and communicate (Schwandt and Marquardt 1999, 206). Tacit knowledge is subconsciously understood and applied, difficult to articulate, developed from direct experience and action and usually shared through highly interactive conversation, storytelling, and shared experience.

Training

The acquisition of knowledge, skills, and competencies intended to improve one's capabilities, productivity, and performance. It forms the core of apprenticeships while also being increasingly used for professional development—to upgrade and update skills throughout one's working life.

REFERENCES

Argyris, Chris, and Donald Schön. 1974. *Theory in Practice: Increasing Professional Effectiveness*. San Francisco: Jossey-Bass.

———. 1978. *Organizational Learning: A Theory of Action Perspective*. Reading, MA: Addison-Wesley.

DuBrin, Andrew J. 2005. *Fundamentals of Organizational Behavior*. 3rd edition. Cincinnati, OH: South-Western College Publishing.

Duhon, Bryant. 1998. "It's All in Our Heads." *Inform* 12 (8): 8–13.

Government of Indonesia, Japan International Cooperation Agency, UN Development Programme, and the World Bank. 2012. "Bali Communiqué by the Co-Organizers, High-Level Meeting "Towards Country-Led Knowledge Hubs." July 10. www.knowledgesharingfordev.org.

Knowles, Malcolm S., Elwood F. Holton III, and Richard A. Swanson. 2012. *The Adult Learner: The Definitive Classic in Adult Education and Human Resource Development*, 7th edition. New York: Routledge.

Lipshitz, Raanan, Victor J. Friedman, and Micha Popper. 2007. *Demystifying Organizational Learning*. Thousand Oaks, CA: Sage Publications.

Nonaka, Ikujiro, and Hirotaka Takeuchi. 1995. *The Knowledge-Creating Company: How Japanese Companies Create the Dynamics of Innovation*. New York: Oxford University Press.

Polanyi, Michael. 1966. *The Tacit Dimension*. Garden City, NY: Doubleday. Chicago: University of Chicago Press, 2009, foreword by Amartya Sen.

Schön, Donald A. 1975. "Deutero-Learning in Organizations: Learning for Increased Effectiveness." *Organizational Dynamics* 4 (1): 2–16.

Schwandt, David R., and Michael J. Marquardt. 1999. *Organizational Learning: From World-Class Theories to Global Best Practices*. Boca Raton, FL: CRC Press.

Senge, Peter, M. 2006. *The Fifth Discipline: The Art and Practice of the Learning Organization*. Revised edition. New York: Crown Publishers.

Zack, Michael H. 1999. "Managing Codified Knowledge." *Sloan Management Review* 40 (4): 45–58.

www.ingramcontent.com/pod-product-compliance
Lightning Source LLC
Chambersburg PA
CBHW060316240426
43661CB00059B/2779